**A QUIET REFLECTION**

# THREADING THE NEEDLES *of* LIFE

Threading The Needles Of Life
Copyright © 2017 by George Byron Crocker

No part of this publication may be reproduced,
distributed, or transmitted in any form or by any
means, including photocopying, recording, or other
electronic or mechanical methods, without the prior
written permission of the author, except in the case
of brief quotations embodied in critical reviews and
certain other non-commercial uses permitted by
copyright law.

Tellwell Talent
www.tellwell.ca

ISBN
978-1-77370-007-6 (Paperback)
978-1-77370-430-2 (eBook)

# AUTHORS NOTES

The idea for this book was born during my darkest day of recovery from a massive stroke and subsequent brain surgery. On the morning of March 27, 2015 I had a massive stroke and then later that afternoon, neurosurgeons had to perform a brain surgery to save my life. The outcome may not have been positive. There was a big possibility I would not survive but I have survived and was inspired to write my story on the pages of this book.

A brain injury is any injury occurring in the brain of any a living organism. Forms and severity of brain injuries can vary greatly, but when symptoms of a brain injury appear it should be addressed immediately.

With limited computer and writing skills, and living with a brain injury, I set out on my new chapter of life, becoming a writer, an author. Writing this book has been a wonderful undertaking and a great help for my recovery from the Acquired Brain Injury (ABI) and recovery from life itself.

When there were ideas in my head during my writing, I had to write it down, write it at that time because I would not remember my writing thoughts the next day or next time I would sit down to write.

At the beginning, it was very difficult to write because my brain would get confused and stressed easily. I soon realized sitting down to write for a time made my damaged brain tired. I needed to shorten my writing sessions and take breaks, go lay down in a quiet room, close my eyes and just rest my brain. The rest period really helped refocus my brain and subside the pain in my head. I was having a problem getting motivated to get going on my project of writing a book, it was a difficult task for me. Lack of motivation is a common problem for brain injury survivors and just one negative word said or misunderstood can cause a brain injury person to become discouraged, and fixate on just that negative thought.

As most people do, I too wanted to avoid difficult tasks. My biggest obstacle was the voice in my head trying to convince me I could not do this, it was telling me to quit. I was not willing to think about quitting, I convinced myself I could do this even if it takes more out of me and more time than I planned, my family cheered me on. Then In the winter of 2017, Nancy and I attended the Alpha program at Saint Benedict's Catholic Church in the Clayton Park section of Halifax. Early in the Alpha program, through prayer and support from others I soon found renewed artistic motivation to get at and finish my project of writing a book. I found renewed energy. I have written my book and completed my project, I pat myself on the back for my perseverance and those that cheered me on, and to Jesus for answering mine and our prayers. Writing a book can be a difficult task; writing a book while living with a brain injury is a very difficult task.

Life can be difficult for most of us, it has been a difficult life for me with the occasional sprinkle of good fortune, but I am still here despite it all. I am thankful for opening my eyes each morning, I have seen the beginning of another day to enjoy being alive on this earth. My first words each morning are, "Thank you God I am here." To get through difficult times in our lives we have to be resilient and, yes, a little stubbornness helps you fight in the face of adversity. The days I was in pain and was cranky are the days I fought the hardest.

When life becomes difficult, at first it is really hard, then we get used to it, then expect it, we lose hope. For brain injury survivors, we usually only have two choices: lose hope and quit or dig in our heels and go forward. We have to believe there is a better life ahead (have the courage to keep trying). "The courage to say I will try again tomorrow." The second you wake up from a brain injury and you are breathing, then every second you live after that you are a Brain Injury Survivor.

After reading this book I believe you will understand my following statement: When I die, please bury me upside down so the world can kiss my ass. But my grave stone will probably say: "Here lays a man at rest who did his best, he tried life and it sure was hard, he did not quit."

My recovery from the (ABI) has been my biggest life challenge. It may also have been the biggest triumph of my life, a life triumphant. Recovery has been slow but steady forward. Every day brings new challenges. Life for some of us always seems to be a struggle. I personally have endured physically and mental abuse, bullying, health curve balls such as a brain injury due to a stroke and brain surgery (ABI). There are also some financial curve balls to endure because of the ABI. My strength of character has seen me through just fine. I did not allow myself to give in to negative self-talk or give up. Victims of a brain injury besides the person with the ABI, are family members, significant others and communities.

> **Quote from Wendy Renzulla**
>
> *"Brain injury survivors are extraordinary people, surviving under the most terrible circumstances, and they are more extraordinary because of it."*

Threading the needles of life is a metaphor for my life. My life has been like trying to thread a needle, in the low light times of a day like dawn or dusk, it is difficult to do.

The important thing is: whatever life throws at you and leaves you in the living population, at the end of each day be brave enough to say what brain injury survivors say: "I will try again tomorrow." That, my friends, is real courage.

Remember these words and if necessary meditate on them: "The further I walk: the further I will see."

# DEDICATIONS

This book is dedicated to my granddaughter, Charlotte Crocker; my son, Stefan Crocker my daughter, Suzanne Crocker; and my girlfriend and best friend, Nancy Irwin. It is all of their love and support that really helped bring me through the ABI and subsequent recovery. Thank you I love you all so much.

To my Fiancé and best friend Nancy

**To my son and daughter**

**Stefan and Suzanne**

**To my Granddaughter Charlotte**

# THREADING THE NEEDLES *of* LIFE

# CHAPTER ONE

*I* had gone through many difficulties in my life. Those difficulties helped form my strength of character, my courage, mental toughness, resiliently, strength, and my undying will to survive, never quit, and pick myself up to carry on no matter what. I would have to draw on all of those attributes that helped prepared me to survive and recover from what was about to happen to me.

> **A quote from Nelson Mandela:**
>
> *"Do not judge me by my successes, judge me by how many times I fell down and got back up again."*

I remember thinking "You have to get the heck up from here George, bye."

I woke up in middle of the night not feeling good, I was still not feeling great at 6 A.M. when my clock alarm rang. I decided to stay back from work that morning, the first time ever not going to work since I started working on the project in November 2011. This was a morning just a few days before my 14-day rotation at the project site was completed. I felt sick to my stomach and generally not great. I did not go to the lodge dining room anytime during the day to eat. Nick and a few others dropped by, knocked on my suite door, voicing their concern for me, asking if I was OK. "Of course," I always answered. "I am doing fine, no problems, I just need to rest I will be ok in the morning." I spent most of the day lying in bed and drifting in and out of sleep. That night I was restless. This continued for another three days, not feeling great but not bad enough to go to a hospital. I thought I had caught a virus that soon would pass. I was talking to Nancy "my girlfriend" over the next few days, she was expressing her concern. On Thursday night, I woke up and noticed my right eye was not working properly, it had closed. When I opened it by force I was seeing double. The next morning my eye was still shut. I was a little worried so I asked the woman on the lodge front desk to take me to a doctor, at the emergency centre in the small nearby town of Witbourne. It was about a half hour drive by car away. It was best not to drive there myself, considering I was not feeling great. Upon arriving at the emergency centre I checked in with reception. After about an hour wait I was called inside to see the doctor, and given a bed/gurney to lay on. Soon a nurse practitioner was checking me over. She noted my blood pressure (BP) was abnormally high, she consulted the doctor, and I was given a BP med and told to wait about half hour then check BP again.

After checking my BP a few times the nurse suddenly stated: "You have to get out of this bed, we need it for somebody else. You will have to wait outside in the waiting room, your BP needs to come down further so we will monitor it again in half hour intervals."

Imagine abnormally high BP and being sent out to a packed waiting room to wait. This is the state of public health care in Canada, at least in Newfoundland; similar stories have been told in provinces all across Canada. The nurse called me inside a couple more times at 20- to 30-minute intervals, to check my BP and I did not feel well enough to argue with her. After another 2 hours, my BP had not stabilized and the nurse then released me with a prescription of BP meds. The nurse should not have done that for sure, she should have ensured I was sent to a hospital for further evaluation. Returning back to the lodge I was not feeling all that great. That evening I was talking to Nancy and she was little worried. After we got off the phone she made a phone call to my brother Freeman in Marystown, NL. On Saturday morning my Nephew Darren, my brother Freeman's son, came to pick me up to drive me to Marystown (my hometown) where I was born. Some of my siblings still lived there. Darren drove me directly to the Burin Peninsula Health Care hospital, near Marystown. At this hospital, I was taken in through emerge after just a few minutes. Immediately the nurse noted my BP was high and needed to come down. The emerge doctor came in to see me, in just a few minutes the nurse administered 5 pills, what those were I do not know but further BP checks revealed my

BP was stabilizing. The doctor also had concern about my right eye. She requested a CT scan. I was soon getting a CT scan. I was later told the results did not reveal anything of concern. I was given a BP med prescription, an appointment to visit an eye doctor on Monday and released to return to the hospital on Monday morning for BP check. On release, I went with my oldest brother Wesley to stay for a few days at his house. I checked my BP three times a day over the weekend. The BP seemed to be stabilized. On Monday, my brother dropped me off at the optometrist to check on my eye. She noted there was damage to the third nerve due to my high BP, and it would correct itself within 4 to 6 weeks.

On Tuesday March 25th I boarded a flight to return to Halifax, Nova Scotia, my home. This may not have been my best idea but thank God I did, considering events to come. Newfoundland is really suffering when it comes to quality of health care. I arrived home to Halifax later that day and Nancy picked me up at the airport. The next couple of days I was feeling ok, but visited my doctor, who prescribed a BP medication. At the time my doctor did not seem worried of any possible complications. The next couple of days I carried on doing my usual routines. Then, at home on the morning of March 27, 2015 just two days after returning home to Halifax, my life and health took a sudden change. Nancy and I got out of bed at about 7 A.M. to get blood testing performed at a local clinic then back home for breakfast. I went to take a shower, Nancy was in the other bathroom I noted as I walked passed the partially closed door on my way to the living room. Normally Nancy went back to her house in the early morning as she ran her business from the home. She worked daily from home. The day before she had decided to bring her laptop with her to my place to work from there the next day. This turned out to be a critical decision on her part, one that probably would save my life considering events to come. As I walked past the bathroom, I was suddenly not feeling right. I went to sit on the couch but sat on the floor instead, and then I collapsed on the floor. I do remember calling to Nancy and trying to push myself up, but my arms would not work, my legs were feeling funny. This is where I remember thinking "You got to the heck up from here George, bye." (The word "bye" is a Newfoundland slang word for boy meaning my friend. Newfoundlanders have a lot of slang words for a lot of things.) I tried as hard as I could but my head felt out of focus, I could not get my weight up, my arms were not working and would not take my weight. On each attempt I would fall back to the floor. Nancy apparently heard me yelling "Nancy! Nancy! Nancy!"

She came running out and saw me on the floor in obvious difficulty. She sprang into action, calling 911 and doing what she could to help me survive. Later, Nancy told me I asked her to just prop me up against the couch and I would be ok. She did not perform that request. She noticed my eyes were rolling back into my head. As I passed out, she was calling 911 a second time, yelling in the phone, "I am losing him you need to get here now!" Soon the paramedics were at our door. I was now passed out. She was worried that when the medics came I would not be able to be revived. She also remembers thinking how she was going to be able to let the paramedics into my apartment building as she did not have my mobile phone password to press the number to open the entrance door (I did not have a land line.) Today was our lucky day as there were people entering the building just as the paramedics arrived, no coincidence I am sure. This was God saying "No worries, I have you George."

The next few hours of my life, God proved many times he had me in his arms. My story for the next day or so is one told to me by my family.

On route to hospital, Nancy, being really emotional, was unable to call my kids so she sent texts Stefan and Suzanne to advise them of my condition and where I was headed via ambulance. This was a call nobody wants to make or receive. Stefan received the call at work on his Blackberry mobile phone, while working on a construction site. While texting, Nancy explained to him I had collapsed on the floor at home. This caused him great concern, and he felt a range of emotions go through his body. Before he could get all the information his phone shut down. This made matters worse for him, especially his emotions. The phone would not restart so he took out its battery and put it back in, (this all took maybe 10 minutes). As soon as possible Stefan called Nancy. She was now at the hospital and, in frantic voices, they exchanged information. Stefan and Suzanne contacted each other. Stefan would have to get her in Eastern Passage where she lived —about a half hour away. Suzanne's car was in the garage, she had dropped it for repairs early that morning. Stefan rushed to get Suzanne. Both of them headed to Halifax to the QEII. As they drove into Halifax they were talking and discussing possible scenarios. At Robbie Street in Halifax matters further went wrong: there was a traffic jam. This worried and frustrated them even more. One can only imagine what was going through their heads as they were trying to get to the hospital, because their dad could be dying or even dead by now. It was very emotional for them.

There was a team of health professionals waiting for Nancy and I when we arrived at the hospital emergency room. I was passed out by this time and not aware of anything. Doctors soon diagnosed me with a massive stroke.

Later I was told that my son and daughter both rushed to the hospital. When they arrived, doctors were working hard to assess my condition and its cause. Stefan and Suzanne said it was the worst day of their lives when they saw me lying on a gurney hooked up to equipment (my eyes almost closed). I do not remember, but Stefan said I looked scared and dazed, not aware of anything. It was really difficult. They said it was difficult to get information out of the doctors, they were non-committal. The question was: What kind of stroke? Drugs could not be administered until they knew the stroke type. The wrong drug could be fatal. Time was of the essence. Nancy followed my gurney. She stayed with me through the testing, as my condition continued to deteriorate. She was frustrated but understood. Time has a whole new meaning when experiencing something like this with a loved one. Testing revealed it was a clot, not a bleed, and I was soon diagnosed with an ischemic stroke (critical information). Hospital staff prepared documents that needed to be signed by my next of kin to allow doctors to administer an anti-blood clotting agent to me to clear the clot. Although Nancy was not my wife yet, they kept calling her my wife, she let it go as she knew time was our enemy. She was told this anti-clotting agent may not work, it could lead to death but it was necessary. Without it doctors said, my quality of life could be minimal or I may not survive at all. Stefan and Suzanne had not yet arrived, she had to make the call. She signed the documents with her own name and signature, they gave me the shot.

Stefan and Suzanne arrived to the shock of seeing their 58 year old father, who was always filled with life, humour, strong and boisterous, lying basically half-dead on a gurney with a huge team of medical staff, wires and tubes around me. They were in shock. The "clot buster drug" as it was affectionately called, worked initially. The anti-blood clotting agent left a possibility of me bleeding out and dying. It helped but did not reverse the effects of the stroke fully. My family were taken aside by doctors, a decision was necessary, permission was required to perform a new type of brain surgery to hopefully solve my condition if I was ever to live, recover and have a chance at any quality of life. Nancy stated to the surgeon "I know you guys like to cut but if this was your wife having to make this decision what you would want her to do?" The surgeon told her "I would want my wife to sign the documents and allow me to have the surgery with a chance at a recovery and some quality of life, perform the surgery." After some discussion, permission was granted and their wait began. Surgery into the brain could lead to my possible dying and very serious side effects, this was possibly my only chance to survive or have any quality of life. The clot had to be removed. The clots were broken down by the clot buster drug into numerous smaller clots that would allow some blood flow. It was a stressful time; hard and big decisions for my family had to be made. They made the right and only decision they could under the circumstances. This was not an easy decision for my family, but the best decision possible.

http://news.heart.org/guidelines-urge-new-approach-
to-treating-worst-strokes/

This website states:

> "Currently, most people arriving in the emergency room with an ischemic stroke will be evaluated to see if the clot can be dissolved by a drug called tissue plasminogen activator (tPA) that is injected into a vein. However, this must be administered within 3 to 4.5 hours of an acute stroke, and isn't effective in breaking down large clots more than half of the time.
>
> The procedure, called Mechanical Thrombectomy, should be done within six hours of acute stroke symptoms, and only after the patient receives tPA, To remove the clot, doctor's thread a catheter through an artery in the groin up to the blocked artery in the brain. The stent opens and grabs the clot, allowing doctors to remove the stent with the trapped clot. Special suction tubes may also be used.

God guided my family's decision and my doctor's hands I am sure. My family were told I may not survive. The carotid artery on my left side was completely ripped. This is where the catheter had to go through in order for an apparatus at the top of the catheter to grab the clots and pull them out through my groin. The surgeon said there was a chance he could make things worse. He could push more clots through; it could rip the artery more. Minutes dragged for them that seemed like hours, waiting to hear any news but expecting the worst. My son would pace the hallways, leave for a few minutes and return. Nancy asked Suzanne, "Where is Stefan going?" Suzanne said, "He can't handle it, he's stepping out to cry." He stepped out many times over the few hours of the surgery.

News came: surgery looked like it was successful, I was alive for now, only recovery time, the next 72 hours would tell for sure. I later learned the type of surgery I needed and received was only available in three places in Canada, Halifax being one of those. I was lucky I had decided to return to Halifax from Newfoundland. Currently this surgery is available in all provinces accept Newfoundland and PEI. God was guiding me to make good decisions. Proverbs 16:9 a man's heart deviseth his way but the lord directeth his steps. I survived and now two and a half years later, I'm doing ok. I'm not fully recovered but getting there, happy to have this extra time on this earth and living this life. A second chance. I am thankful each day I wake up to see another day. To have the opportunity to share more days with my children, my granddaughter, and my girl Nancy. They are all truly amazing. I am a lucky man

# CHAPTER TWO

My immediate family also later advised my siblings who are spread across other provinces of Canada; they were kept updated via posts on Facebook. Now I admit I am no fan of Facebook, I do not and have never had an account, but here is the one time I know of it being used properly: with my worried family being so large and spread across Canada. Suzanne took on the role of setting up a Facebook page so all could be kept informed of my condition and progress. The constant talking on the phone was exhausting. Suzanne, Nancy and Stefan wanted to put their complete focus on me, not focus on my brothers and sisters concerns. So, regularly during the day Suzanne updated the Facebook page, answering any messages and concerns, a job she did so well, and it was much appreciated by everyone.

I was in hospital for 90 ninety days. I had three weeks at the QEII under acute care, then I was transferred to Nova Scotia Rehabilitation hospital for further recovery. Nancy and Stefan would be my constant evening or day companion, depending on circumstances. Suzanne came to visit as often as she could; she also found it difficult to see me as I was. She did have a small child at home. The only times Stefan and Nancy did not visit were a few evenings when they had a flu and did not want me to catch it. Sometime after surgery I opened my eyes and looked at my most important assets sitting at my bedside: Suzanne, Stefan and Nancy, all waiting and hoping I would wake and be ok. Nobody knew for sure what the outcome would be. I was now a brain injury survivor.

I also want to make an important note: my ex-wife Sharon's two sisters, Veronica and Ita, were at my bedside also when I woke up. They had come to support my children and Nancy at this critical time. Apparently as soon as they were advised of my condition they rushed to the QEII to support Suzanne, Stefan and Nancy and do anything necessary to help. I thank them for that and ask God to bless them. I had a good relationship with them during their younger years, the time when both were growing up into the women they are today, with their own families.

As I opened my eyes, I did not know much about what was going on but knew immediately I was in trouble. I had tubes hooked to me. I was gently informed of my condition. Apparently, the carotid artery in my neck had been torn. Doctors did not know when or how the trauma to the artery happened, neither do I. The blood clot had formed in the artery, eventually releasing and going to my brain. Doctors had removed the clots that were causing a life threatening stroke condition. My blood pressure when I arrive at ER was 180/146: lucky to be alive, it was said. A miracle a doctor would say in later days. If my BP was over 180 I would not have been able to receive the clot buster drug. After I woke up doctors and nurses soon came to my bedside asking many questions. Nancy thought it frustrating the barrage of questions the doctors and specialists would ask both at the beginning of my hospital stay and the next few weeks. She understood they were necessary but her quarrel was the questions came at such a rapid speed even she could not keep up with them. How could a person with a new brain injury keep up? I could not remember how to tell the time or what day it was. It seemed strange to me for them to be asking so many questions and at such a fast pace because my brain could not focus well. Doctors need to understand, although they may see many patients a year with a stroke, to the family and the patient this is all new; do not ask questions so rapidly just take your time. Give the patient time to think and respond.

I soon knew I could barely move my left arm or leg, and had no feeling in them. I could move my arm a little from the shoulder only and my leg a little from the hip only, but I did not panic. I, for some reason, felt at peace. I soon drifted back to sleep for another day or so. I learned later from my family that they were told I could not walk and they were not sure when I would be able to. When I woke later, the first question I was asked was, "What time is it?" There was a clock on the wall across from my bed. I did know the time then, and apparently this was big deal for my family, the doctors and nurses. I was also informed I would not be allowed to eat solid food because there was a worry about choking they said; a swallow test was ordered. If that failed I would have to be fed by a feeding tube; nurses and visitors had to be careful with me. They could not give me any solid food — even all pills were to be ground up and added to apple sauce, and fed to me carefully with a spoon for now, until I could get further testing. The test proved positive and I could have solid food, but no real food for a few days. When I was allowed to eat what was referred to as "real" hospital food, it was horrible. Of course, this was partly due to the fact I was placed on a sodium free diet, or "tasteless diet" as I referred to it. Cooks in public hospitals must have to take courses to learn how to make the most tasteless and crappy food for patients. I really enjoyed the food when my family brought me in some home cooking that had some taste but no sodium.

My family eventually went home to rest and sleep; they needed it. Nancy had stayed for 48 hours just placing two straight back chairs together. In the middle of one night I woke up, I was alone and wanted to pee badly so I got myself out of bed. I remember my legs felt so heavy and weak, like iron. I hit my buzzer on my wrist, for the nurse, I could barely stand. The nurse came in and asked, "Why you are out of bed? You cannot walk!"

"Well, I have been walking since I was a kid. I know I can walk, ha-ha," I stated.

With that, she said, "Get your shoes on, you have to keep walking."

Jesus had me in his arms again, taking care of me. The nurse placed her arms underneath mine to prop me up and walk with me. I did walk although not very well. This was a big deal it seemed, apparently a pathway had opened from my brain to my legs. The nurse knew this and was trying to ensure it continued. The doctor on duty came in to give me a good check over that lasted for what was at least an hour. He pronounced I had increased feelings in my arm and legs, for now. I passed out again and went back to sleep. For the next few days and weeks I would sleep a lot. I would have many more doctor visits to my bed for checks in the days to come. When my family were informed of my progress it was a happy occasion for all. My first hurray moment was a positive start to recovery. It was a celebration moment and I have been walking since that moment. Sometimes I didn't walk well and sometimes I had to use a wheelchair, but I mostly walked around the hospital area where I was stationed and that is what is important. My family was very happy, this was the start of my long recovery process and it's been two and a half years now and counting.

Nancy told me she will never forget the first time she saw me walk after the stroke. It had seemed bleak to her after nurses had brought her a large booklet to read to prepare herself for what could happen after a stroke and subsequent surgery. Things such as continued paralysis, walking with a cane, a walker or not walking at all, a wheel chair, severe memory issues, personality changes, inability to live independently, etc. I have had none or very little of those effects.

Even today, two and a half years later, I still have leg pain and stiffness that only limits my activities; these leg issues are only just now starting to subside somewhat. Eventually I will get to a full recovery, maybe not fully, but will have to learn to accept this new version of me. My physical condition was and is compromised for now. I must continue to move forward and not give up no matter what.

When my co-workers were informed of my condition they were very surprised because they thought — considering how careful I was with what I ate and how I exercised regularly — I would be the last person a stroke would happen to. I received cards and fruit baskets from my co-workers. Recovery is difficult, but I am recovering, thank God for that. Although at times now, I may not appear to have a brain injury I still live with a brain injury that gives me new challenges every day: lack of focus, inability to comprehend as I could before, unable to concentrate. I was visited by a speech pathologist soon after reviving from the surgery and my constant sleeping patterns. I was soon also visited by an occupational therapist. The speech pathologist told Nancy that she was concerned because I had garbled speech. I had developed an accent that was difficult to understand. Nancy stated he does not, his speech is perfectly normal he is a Newfoundlander. What does a speech pathologist from Ontario know, I thought? My BP was soon stabilized with medication and I was improving. During those first few days and for many more Nancy and Stefan were my constant bedside companions. They were real angels.

# CHAPTER THREE

*I* was born in the mid-1950s. To our younger generation, that is so long ago. To me it seems only yesterday; time passes quickly, faster it seems as one gets older. I was born to a woman who was very abusive to us children, both mentally and physically.

I am a descendant of John Crocker who emigrated by boat from Bridge Port England to Newfoundland in the late mid-1800s. Upon arriving he applied for and acquired title to a large block of land in Creston South/Mortier Bay/Placentia Bay Newfoundland.

John, as his grave stone states, was born in 1829, died at Creston South NL in 1913 at age 84.

The information I have states John was deeded land in Creston South, Newfoundland as follows: from the edge of a brook on the west known as the Mill Brook and on the North along the high water's edge of Creston Inlet of Mortier Bay to the South along the community road, then to the east and along the edge of Murley's Brook. On land near Murley's Brook, an Anglican church would be built that included a cemetery. Many head stones in this cemetery have the name Crocker engraved on them, including those of my grandparents and great grandparents.

Cod drew seasonal fisherman from southern England to Newfoundland in the 1700s and 1800s. Some decided to resettle in Canada permanently when southern England experienced crop failures, unemployment and overpopulation. In the 1800s, Newfoundlanders expanded from cod to other industries such as seal hunting, shipbuilding, fur trapping, and shipping and retail business owners. Eventually, overfishing depleted the market, forcing some to move to Nova Scotia to work in factories and the Cape Breton coal mines; others moved to New England's coastal towns like Boston and Providence to find work. Newfoundland has a long relationship with Boston and Providence, and many Newfoundland women and men married partners from those areas, eventually raising families there or both returning to Newfoundland to raise families.

John Crocker stayed in Newfoundland. He was a fisherman who would marry Mary Fizzard of Creston North at Creston Inlet, Mortier Bay. Mary died of Tuberculosis (TB) at just a young age — only in her twenties. John later married Ann Riggs of Burin, NL. They had eight children, one of which was a son name of Eli, born in 1876. who would later become my Grandfather.

Newfoundland was not part of Canada but a colony of England at this time. A Canadian province would come later in 1949 as a result of what many say was a rigged vote orchestrated by the governments of England and Canada. England wanted to get forgiveness from Canada for the war debt she owed, and Canada wanted Labrador's mineral rights to support the central Canadian factories, so it is said the deal was made. England would deliver Newfoundland to Canada, as did happen in 1949. Until 1949, Newfoundland was pretty much on its own except for the meddling of the English government. I could now go on about how England took advantage of Newfoundland, but information on this is documented in many ways including the book, "Don't Tell the Newfoundlanders "Author, Greg Malone and other places where history is recorded. I will refrain from telling it in my words to not deviate from the story I want to tell in this book.

I make no apology for my steadfast belief Canada needs to rid itself of any attachment to the Britain tourist attraction called "The Royal Family", or as I also call them, "The Entitled and Pompous Group." The Royals are Winsor's, a German bloodline, not British. Why does a sovereign nation such as Canada need or have a foreign monarch as head of state? It should be sent packing ASAP. While most countries try to hang on or achieve their independence, Canada wants to hang on to having a foreign monarchy that has long out lived its usefulness all over the world. Bye, bye and good riddance I say. When can I actually vote to send them packing? Most Canadian politicians do not have the balls to do the right things; they just want to hang onto power, their government cheque and their pension.

Although times were harsh and difficult in Newfoundland in the 1800s John did carve out a life farming and fishing there. Although many of his descendants have now moved to other parts of Canada and the world, many also still live on the land he owned in Creston South. As for me, I was born there in Creston South to a poor family, at my parents' house, not a hospital.

In Creston South, we did not have electricity until 1962, six years after I was born. At this time, the house light was provided by kerosene lamps and sometimes candles fashioned from the wax that was removed from bologna skins. The year-round available heat was provided by a woodstove, only. I remember my siblings using the lamp to do school home work. There were no street lights. People used a battery-operated flash light to travel about after dark. In my youth, I remember our house and many others had no indoor plumbing; we just had an outhouse for toilet facilities. In the middle of the night if you needed to go, the men and boys had to go outside and down the path to the outhouse using a flash light. The girls got to stay inside using a chamber pot stored beneath the bed for those occasions. I remember being so scared going to the outhouse in the middle of the night, I could crap in my pants along the way. I went to the outhouse only if I really could not hold until dawn, sometimes it was a restless, sleepless night trying not to go, other times I'd just go check the girls room; if they were asleep, I'd go there. As a child, you will try anything to avoid going out in the dark in the middle of the night. A child's imagination runs wild outside in the dark night. Of course, being boys and having brothers, on occasion one brother would go out and hide nearby just to scare whomever came out to the outhouse first. So it was a good idea to check if all brothers were in bed before going out.

The Marystown area had only a dirt road for many years of my youth, no paved roads. The town was divided into the north side and the south side by Mortier Bay and the Creston Inlet water way. There was no bridge until after Confederation with Canada; until then access was by boat only. A local politician was said to have worked hard to get it built. Has any politician ever worked hard, really? Politicians are usually only speaking the truth when they are not talking, but sometimes they actually do get something accomplished.

All my brothers, sisters and I were delivered at birth by a midwife in the house my father built, born on land that had been owned and worked by the Crocker's family for generations. It is said as a joke some were born in bed while others were dropped somewhere between the washing tub and the clothesline.

I was born the 9th child of 12. My family included fifteen: five boys, seven girls, three step-sisters. The three older step-sisters were from my father's first marriage, plus 2 parents, wow. Imagine that: 15 kids plus parents, in a poor family. My half-sisters had left home before I was born as they just needed to get away from the abusive step mother. They told me this on many occasions, but for some reason those that lived in nearby towns occasionally came back for Sunday dinners, especially Mildred. She told me later in life she just wanted to see dad and her other brothers and sisters, check on them see how they were doing.

My oldest sisters (my step-sisters) were born to my father and his first wife, Sofia Murray. Sofia died of TB as a young woman, a killer in those days. These three sisters also told me stories of their step-mother — my mother's — abusiveness and cruelty.

Sofia' death at a young age is a sad story. My father's sister, Pearl, had contracted TB from her husband's father while caring for him. After getting TB she soon died as a very young woman. My father's first wife Sofia was caring for Pearl and she also contracted TB and died as a result. TB was a huge killer in Newfoundland during this time in history and sometimes wiping out whole families was very common.

On a tragic note, Mildred, known affectionately as Millie by her siblings, was in hospital on her death bed. She was dying with cancer in her mid-60s. Laying in hospital she told me, you know I love you like you were one of my own. I also told her I loved her so much, always had. Millie was such a kind, loving woman. She always had a smile and a kind word for all; she was and is a real angel. My brother told me that, while on her death bed, Millie said, "If your mother, Violet, wants to come visit me I would like to forgive her for the things she did to me as a child." But my mother refused to go visit her. Imagine that!!

All of my family were raised in a three-bedroom house; sleeping arrangements were cramped at best. My parents would have been too busy for Social Media, Internet or mobile phones if those things were around back then. Parents and children today are busy texting, and using the Internet and Social Media. The best thing folks can do to free up some real time is to have their phones amputated from their hands. How did we get to make our lives so public anyway? I refer to the current generation as the "Social Media Bunch," always wanting to interfere in others' business. They seem to believe free speech is only their right and not those they disagree with. A person who forgets to take their mobile phone with them, and realizes their phone is left in the car or at home acts like a dog having separation anxiety from its owner. People are so addicted to their cell phones now, I think mobile phones now own people, not people owning the phone anymore.

There is steadfast rules at our house: limited texting during the day and no cell phones are invited to dinner, just people. Guess what happens at dinner when somebody asks how was your day? A real person to person conversation happens. I grew up in a time when people had real things to do and shared real time and had real conversations with real people, real kids and real spouses. I guess that is my Social Media and mobile phone addiction rant.

As boys, our childhoods, our characters, our values, our beliefs were controlled and formed by a woman called mom. As boys, we were told "Big boys do not cry. Boys have to be strong." We were told that crying or showing emotion was a weakness. Tell a child something often enough they will soon believe and carry it forward through life. I heard the lie boys do not cry, boys have to be strong many times growing up. Even today many years later I have a problem showing emotion; I see it as a sign of weakness. Girls were never told not to cry but are cuddled and tears wiped away when they cried. Why the contradiction by mothers? My son was never told that lie.

I believe showing emotion and crying on occasion is just fine, although it is difficult for me. I remember getting a beating from my mother. If I cried, I would get a worse beating for crying, "Shut up or you will get more," she would shout.

During meal times my mother would sit with a leather belt over her shoulder. Any child that spoke got a quick swat on the shoulder, head or face, whatever part she happened to reach with it when she made a swing with that leather belt.

My sisters tell me most of the housework in our house was done by the girls, not mother. Mother would sit in her rocking chair mostly giving orders. If things were not done correctly a beating would have to be taken. They were as I was, very fearful of her. She did not show any positive reinforcement, affection or love to us children.

I remember Saturday morning all us boys were sent out of the house. We had outside chores that needed doing the same on all weekdays except Sunday, because Sunday was the Sabbath day, it was to be kept holy, absolutely no work to be performed on Sundays. The weekday chores were making firewood, cutting hay, cleaning the hen house, killing and cleaning two chickens for Sunday dinner, tending the horses and cleaning the barn, and tending vegetable gardens. My sisters cleaned the house, and washed and waxed the thin canvas that covered the wooden floors. They also baked cookies or maybe a cake and a pie, peeled veggies and did preparation for Sunday dinner. These baking chores were completed after washing and waxing floors, but not before laying out cardboard boxes that were taken apart and spread to ensure the floor stayed clean for Sunday. Later in the day after us boys were allowed back inside we were usually given woolen socks to pull on to shine the waxed floors. Nothing was allowed to be done on Sunday for it was Gods day a holy day; all kids were expected to go to church. Going to church was of no harm to us but I hated it then because most of my friends did not have to go. They were outside playing and having fun, and I was teased about having to go to church. I now know it was probably the best thing for a kid to do to learn about the teaching of Jesus and some morals. After I became an adult I continued going to church, mostly with my wife Sharon and our kids as often as possible. Other times or I just went alone. I have always felt it was special to attend a church service with my wife and kids. After my divorce later in life, I continued going to church alone or with my girlfriend or partner; it was and is important to me. Church makes me feel a since of community and of love toward our God.

The Farewell family across Crocker Lane also went to church on Sunday. They went to the United Church or sometimes the Salvation Army with their father, and also Sunday school as the Crocker's did. I still remember many of the bible teachings at Sunday school while attending at the Salvation Army or United churches. Most of the kids in my community that did not go to church — to my recollection and knowledge —did not go grow up to have good morals, but it seemed to me they also got more love and fewer beatings than me. The Crocker and Farewell families were taught good morals by parents and grandparents. We were taught the Ten Commandments, good morals, and things like: no fighting, say kind words about neighbours, don't drink alcohol or smoke, stay away from drugs, and be kind to others. We were given lots of guilt, as church indoctrination does, with a lot of man-made church rules not bible teachings, as is common in most religions. The church preachers of the day preached sermons about fearing God and, as was the common theme of churches, the end is near. Only later in life did I realize God is not meant to be feared but loved by all, including me. My role is to love the God figure back as he loved me. Currently I note, of all the Crocker kids not one smoke or does drugs and most have a few drinks of alcohol only for social occasions.

# CHAPTER FOUR

I do not remember a lot of my grandmother Adelaide Hillier, my mother's mother. She died when I was really young. I do note some of her life was similar to my own, so include her story as I know it for part of this book. I remember she lived with my mother's sister, Rebecca, and her husband, Levi, and family; we called them Aunt Becky and Uncle Levi. Grandmother came to our house every Sunday after morning church and for the big dinner that was had in all Newfoundland homes at noon on Sundays. She usually stayed for the day. I remember sometimes I had to go to church with her to the Salvation Army. She had a rule to behave in church: talking or any bad behavior was not tolerated. I always behaved well for her it seems, probably due to the respect for her by me and all my family members. Most of what I know about Grandmother Hillier was as told to me by my siblings and cousins. I remember a few things. She was a happy woman although she had a rough life. On the Sunday visits she liked to sit in the rocking chair in our house singing hymns.

When she was a little girl, Grandmother Hillier's father, Enoch Murley, made a living fishing, farming and raising some animals for food. There were also many fruit trees on the property. Grandmother's own mother's name was Anne. After grandmother's birth, her mother did not recover well, she died from complications.

There were no hospitals to go for births of children, just a mid-wife was available. Her mother left behind a daughter, my grandmother, at two years old, and an older son John and his twin sister, Mary.

After her mother died, grandmother's father, Enoch, was away much of the time tending fishing and other necessary things needed to survive the harsh late 1800s and early1900s. Grandmother was dearly loved by her mother, so now with mom gone the stable influence of mom was missing and big changes were in store for her and her siblings. Within a year after Anne's death, Enoch married a local widow, Caroline. Traumatic events were about to happen to grandmother and her siblings. Caroline was a very unkind and abusive step-mother. They were often cold, hungry, neglected and severely punished for even the smallest of wrongs. In those days, their father was away a lot ensuring the family was taken care of, doing what had to be done to survive, it seems he did not know of the abuse, was not aware or just too busy to interfere. The woman were usually left to running the house in those days and the men did not interfere with that, but left them to do what was necessary. Child rearing was left to the woman as well. Enoch was like most men in those days, he was emotionally detached and distant from children. There was no comfort for the children from their father.

Caroline, a widow, had emotional problems and brought pain and suffering along with her own children to the marriage. She had little time for Enoch's children from his first marriage. She probably married Enoch out of necessity to survive, not for any kind of love.

Things did not improve after Enoch and Caroline had two sons of their own, Enoch Jr. and Thomas. Thomas died of a lung issue, possibly TB, about a year later, and Enoch died at age five of scarlet fever. These events really aggravated Caroline and her hostile feelings toward Enoch's children from his first marriage grew worse. She became engrossed in her own self-pity and was very negative indeed. Enoch became even more distant from Caroline and his children. Events I am told became very bad. My grandmother was abused physically and mentally, her parents were very neglectful of the children. Grandmother lost her innocence in not a nice way I am told, but the details have not been revealed to me. It probably was too horrible to tell, and maybe best for me not to know. I am told she was also abused with sticks and belts by her step-mother Caroline for almost no reason. Once her bare bottom was burned on the stove for wetting the bed.

In 1901, after a severe beating from Caroline, grandmother was left at the low water's mark at the edge of Creston Inlet and told to stay there until the tide came up so she would drown and be taken away. The pain and suffering of this little girl is unimaginable. She sat there on a cold rocky beach, crying from the rejection and the physical and emotional pain of having done nothing to deserve this cruel treatment. I am sure she felt abandoned and in absolute terror as the tide began to rise. As she lay on the beach, a woman, Aunt Anne Mayo, who was walking home, heard a child crying so went to check it. I think Aunt Anne was my grandfather Eli Crocker's sister who was married to Samuel Mayo Aunt Anne recognized the young girl as Enoch's youngest child Adelaide. She had bruises on her face and arms, probably from a beating. On hearing the girl's story she took Adelaide home with her. Aunt Anne was an angel sent to save my grandmother's life. She kept Adelaide with her in her own house for some time. There was no query from her father or step mother as to her whereabouts. She was not reported missing it seems, and this leads me to think her parents — or at least her stepmother — were happy to get rid of her. This cruelty was never forgotten by Grandmother, but she forgave, although forgetting was impossible.

Aunt Anne and Sam had a large family of their own and could not care long-term for Adelaide. They spoke with the church minister about the situation. The clergy spoke about it in church on a Sunday morning. A family of Broydells, Henry and his wife, reached out to help. They had only one son, Ralph, age 13, and they would raise them both as brother and sister. My grandmother was about to have a little more pleasantness in her life, saved by the grace of God and some good Godly folks. Some years later, Grandmother established a relationship with her siblings and her father, forgiving but never forgetting. Addie and her father never did have a meaningful relationship after that. My grandmother taught us the importance of forgiving and moving on in life. If she could forgive what she went through, then I can do it also.

On December 17, 1913, my grandmother married Thomas Hillier of Lance L'eau, located on the shores of an ocean harbour known as Burin Bay. There were no roads to Lance L'eau, just a horse path from the small town of Epworth or by boat. Thomas was a young, unmarried man of 22 years old. Grandmother was happy with a man she loved and was living in a community where she was accepted and loved. She was a kind, happy woman with joy in her heart despite her childhood. Soon they would have some children, Rebecca, Violet (my mother), Muriel, Gordon, and one miscarriage. Grandmother was a devoted Christian and loved God. She went to church regularly with all the family, but tragedy was never far off.

At 35 years old in 1926, my grandfather, Thomas, contracted TB. He continued to work at fishing and provide for his family the best he could with some help from local fisherman. On one Sunday morning after eating a Sunday dinner, he was sitting on the veranda overlooking Lance L'eau when he began to haemorrhage heavily. As friends and family looked on he would bleed to death, there was nothing they could do to help him at this time. My mother

Violet was just four years old at the time. She was just close to home coming from a friend's house when she saw her father's lifeless body being taken inside by family members and family friends.

The future now being faced by grandmother and her children was very bleak. Grandfather Hillier had been a successful fisherman, so grandmother was considered well off at that time, but all that changed in a heartbeat. Grandmother sank into poverty and despair, she did not have much money. When a woman did not have a man to earn a livelihood at this time in Newfoundland history, things usually did not go well for the family. Very soon the family was dependent on welfare, known as the "dole" (a small stipend of money provided by the government of England). The family had never been on the dole but knew others in the community that were, and knew it was a hard life. There was no help for housing costs, no money for coal or wood; the dole was for food only, not even enough for that, really. It was $1.80 per person per month from the British Government. Newfoundland was a colony of England at the time.

The family soon became accustomed to hand-me-down clothes, when they were available. Cloth made from flour sacks and brim bags were common. (Brim bags were a perforated cloth bag commonly used in those days for sacks to store or carry potatoes. The holes allowed the vegetables to breathe and avoid quick rotting.) Grandmother once went to request the welfare or dole officer change some of her molasses orders to butter but was sworn at by him and told to be thankful for what she was getting. She walked away in tears and worry for her three children. Grandmother bravely carried on, and partly because of the help of family and friends they survived. The English did not seem to care if they survived or nor, which was typical of English sentiment toward Newfoundland at the time. Tragedy, devastation and hardship was not yet over for my grandmother.

A tsunami hit the south coast of Newfoundland on November 18, 1929 at about 5 P.M. It was the result of a major earthquake that occurred approximately 250 km south of Newfoundland along the southern edge of the Grand Banks. This magnitude 7.2 tremor was felt as far away as New York and Montreal, and recorded as far away as Lagos, Portugal (some 4,060 km away).

Over the years as a child I heard many stories about the tidal wave. It was said that about two hours after the earthquake, the tidal wave struck the southern end of the Burin Peninsula in Newfoundland, and this included the small fishing village of Lance L'eau where my Grandmother Hillier lived. Three main pulses came, causing local sea levels to rise between two and seven metres or as locals at the time said, between 6 and 20 feet. The waves were higher than the houses. At the heads of several of the long narrow bays on the Burin Peninsula the momentum of the Tsunami carried water as high as 13 metres or 40 feet as told by locals. This giant sea wave claimed a total of 28 lives, 27 of whom drowned on the Burin Peninsula. Another died in 1933 from her injuries that were sustained from the earthquake. The day after the tsunami, a winter storm hit the Burin Peninsula hard, dropping temperatures and adding sleet and snow to the survivors' misery. It was tough, some with no shelter, huddling in other homes or sheds that were not damaged badly and many without a heat source. Most cut firewood normally located in people's yards that had been washed away by the tidal wave. Help took about three days to arrive from the capital of St John's. Immediate help came from local town's folks. Many fishing villages that were not destroyed would rebuild and some continue to exist even today.

Although Grandmother's house was close to the beach, all the family escaped uninjured, but the village was devastated. Some residents hung on for a while but currently this little fishing village does not exist at all, it has disappeared. After the tsunami local fishing was devastated for a few years. Most residences moved to nearby towns and villages around the area.

In 1992, I made a boat trip to visit the area where the village of Lance L'eau was once located, a visit of mixed emotions. Very few remnants of any structures or signs life of a previous and proud fishing village is left to find. I stood on the shore where I believed was the land where my grandparents and family once lived. I felt a sadness for them, and tried to think about and understand what must have been endured here. I asked the question, "Why did they have to have to endure such hardship and difficulty?" As I stood there I could not help but shed a tear for the prosperous times that turned into suffering and hardship, of what they must have went through in this little village, then I heard my grandmother's voice say, "No time for tears, it will get you no-where." I nodded my head and smiled and as I got back into the boat and looked back towards land, I was thinking I could be the last of her descendants to ever return here. I would like future generations to know their heritage and to understand the strength of character of Adelaide Hillier, my grandmother.

After the tsunami and the devastation of her home and community, Grandmother moved to the small nearby town of Levin's Cove to live. She took up residence with her acquired brother Ralph, the son of the family who had cared for her after Aunt Anne Mayo found a home for her when her step mother Caroline had left her at the water's edge to drown. Grandmother and her children were happy as could be living with Ralph who was very kind to them. Ralph worked at a local family mill. To her daughters, Ralph was known as Uncle Ralph. Ralph had a daughter, Susie, and a son, Joe. Ralph's wife had died from complications of giving birth to Joe, and Ralph would die in the 1950s of colon cancer. Grandmother and Joe continued to live in the family home until Joe drowned in a boating accident during a trip in the area known locally as the Fresh Pond. The rest of Grandmother's life is difficult also, overcoming tragedy and hardship alike, but the family did do ok overcoming tragedy as it arose and bravely carried on. Later in life Grandmother went to live with her daughter, Rebecca, known by us as Aunt Becky, in Creston South. By this time all her children had been married and had homes and families of their own.

I remember as a young boy going to Aunt Becky's house on many occasions to visit Grandmother Hillier or Nan Hillier as she was affectionately known. Although she had come through many hard times she never complained and was never abusive. She was a kind, loving person who had great faith in God, up to her dying day. Grandmother had an ABI caused by a stroke in 1962, that took away some of her quality of life. She died of a second stroke in 1967.

After the initial stroke, her life became more difficult. Health care in most Newfoundland out port towns was virtually non-existent at this time in history, except for some home remedies. The English government did not care enough about Newfoundland's people to give a darn about them. Now you may have more understanding of my dislike for England and the Royals.

When I listen I can still hear my grandmother Hillier singing hymns on Sunday afternoons while sitting in the rocking chair near the wood stove at my childhood home. She lived a brave life and was a strong woman that never gave up no matter what life threw at her. Life did throw many challengers at her, more than most, but at the end of each day she always had the courage to say: "I will try again tomorrow," and she always did. She had no quit. She did not know that feeling or that word. She is the bravest and the most courageous person I have personally known.

My Grandmother Crocker, on my dad's side, came to live with us when I was a young boy. I do not have any memories of my Grandfather Crocker. My Grandfather Eli died before

I was born. The Crocker grandparents lived on Crocker's meadows, on land previously owned by my great Grandfather John Crocker. My Grandfather Eli had built a two story house on the land for a home to live in and raise a family, with his wife, my Grandmother Edith. They had seven children: four sons and three daughters. Leonard, Thomas, Rose, Pearl, Harold, Edith and my father, Archibald, were their names. Harold and Edith died as children. Of course, the name Rose was fitting. My grandmother always loved roses, as did my step sister Blanch who could never have too many roses in her garden at her home in Toronto where she lived from the 1950s until her death of cancer in 2016. I also like roses, as does my granddaughter, Charlotte. Grandmother planted and grew many wild rose bushes around the family home in Creston South. When in bloom the fragrance from the roses filled the house through the open doors and windows in the summer. The meadows had vegetable gardens for food, and grass that grew high to be cut for hay to feed horses and other animals they had. Animals were used for food for the family, not pets. They carved out a living farming and fishing. Grandmother was a quiet woman, but always happy, it seemed. Life was not easy in those days.

When I was a boy, I noticed most Crocker's I knew were light-haired and fair-skinned except my family. My family and extended family have darker skin, and black or dark hair. It was said my Grandmother Crocker was of Spanish descent, but I have discounted that information. I recently provided a DNA sample to Ancestry DNA. The results show my ancestry ethnicity estimate is 66% Great Britain, 18% Greece/Italy, 25% Northern Europe. I do know my Grandmother Crocker came from Burin NL, she had the name of Edith Beazley.

I do remember she had darker skin pigmentation, like Spanish or Italian or something similar. Growing up I did know some folks with the Beazley last name who lived in Burin. They were relatives of Grandmother's, and were also of darker skin, similar to Spanish or Italian. I do not have any information on my grandmother's extended family or heritage.

Now Eli was a tough, strong type of fellow, not very emotional. He was typical for men in those days, as they were attributes required for survival, to provide for and raise a family. Eventually he built a schooner to use for carrying goods up and down the southeast coast of Newfoundland with his brother. Thomas had his own schooner. They continued this way of life until one day, while returning from St. John's with a full load during a strong wind, tragedy would strike. Thomas was at the wheel at the stern of the schooner near the rudder when a full gust from the strong wind took the sails jib in full force causing it to release and swing around fast and violently hitting him in the upper body. Before he could react, he was knocked overboard. My grandfather's boat was in the lead, so he and his crew saw this happening but due to the strong wind, my grandfather could not save Thomas even though he tried as best he could. He had disappeared from site and was never found. He was listed as drowned at sea. My grandfather did not sail the schooner again after that but continued to fish, going out daily in his smaller boat, weather permitting, for the inshore fishery. He also continued with the farming and raising animals

There were also the daily chores of tending gardens and animals along with his three sons Lenard, Thomas and Archibald, who were by now grown into young men. Rose helped her mother with the house chores. Grandfather Eli died at age 71 in 1947, it is thought he had dementia at the time of his death. Older folks I talked to some years ago told me my grandfather Crocker was strong and as tough as nails.

Grandmother Edith lived alone after Eli's death until she decided to go live with her son, my uncle Thomas Crocker. My father's brother and family eventually came to live with our family when I was just a young boy. Senior citizens were not placed in long term care homes back then in Newfoundland, they were cared for by family members, a loving, caring family. I really loved Grandmother. She was a warm, strong, classy woman that liked a little shot of brandy once in a while. I remember sitting at her bedside listening to her as she told me many stories about her growing up and about many Crocker's I did not know or meet because they had died years before I was born. I still remember portions of stories she told me, but many have faded with time. She would also occasionally play the piano accordion alone or accompanied by my dad playing his button accordion. The whole family just loved to hear them play. The piano accordion was a bulky heavy instrument, heavy for any average size person, even more so for a small old woman to handle and play it well. Grandmother accomplished both very well, not even breaking a sweat.

I have a large photo of my grandmother and grandfather that was taken on their wedding day in 1908 hanging on my wall, still in its original frame. Grandmother had it hanging on her bedroom wall and had told me I could have it when she was gone. My grandmother Crocker died in 1969 at 89 years old, a good life. It was a sad day indeed, but as in good Newfoundland character we try not to mourn a life too much. We celebrate the life a person had, have a drink, play some music, tell stories about them, talk about their life, and celebrate the life lived.

Tears are not for the dead person — they do not need them. Tears are for one's self because you will miss them or because you did not say to them the things you wish you had when they were alive and had the opportunity to do so. I remember the story a fellow told me. His mother was dying and he was crying. The mother looked up and said, "My son I do not need tears now, it is too late for that, I am going to a better place, enjoy your life and be happy my son, I will see you on the other side."

I only know stories of Grandfather Crocker as told by others from their point of view. Grandfather, I am told, he did not like my mother when he met her and he did not want her around his grandchildren, my step-sisters. Maybe he sensed she was not a kind woman. In later years, I heard my step-sisters speak of the abuse they went through at the hands of Violet. My grandmother never remarried after Eli died. Widows not remarrying was very common in this time in history. On one occasion, while sitting in her rocking chair at her bedside, I asked her about why she did not marry again. "There was nobody who could replace your grandfather," she replied. No need to try. She told me life is short, it soon passes and then it is our turn to meet our God. She said just go to the cemetery and read headstones that tell the year a person was born and year they died. "That dash between those dates is short, it represents how short life really is," she said. A wise woman.

George's Grandfather and Grandmother
Crocker on their wedding day in 1908.

# CHAPTER FIVE

I remember as a child having nightmares. I would wake scared and crying. Instead of cuddling me, and showing me love, understanding or kindness, my mother gave me a beating, and put me back to bed. No love of any kind. I suppose a person cannot give what they do not have. I also remember my brother and I in bed at night laughing and talking. The bedroom door would fly open, my mother would enter already in one of her tirades, holding a mop, broom or a leather belt in her hands — or even a piece of split wood. She would start hitting us with all her strength, with whatever she had in her hands, yelling "You shut up or I'll kill you!" Of course we would cry because the beatings hurt. We had bruises the next day on our face, arms, legs and back but nobody asked about it or cared. These beating happened on many occasions.

On different occasions my mother gave away two of my sisters to other families. They were usually Salvation Army clergy who did not have kids, but wanted some kids or for slaves to do housekeeping chores maybe. My father was usually away working during these times. After dad returned home it seems my sisters returned home again soon after. The amazing thing is, those people actually agreed to take them. Maybe they knew what mother was doing and were just doing a favour to the children to get them away from her.

One sister told me that when she was about nine she was sent away to Green's Harbour NL, about 200 miles away, to live with a Salvation Army clergy.

To get to Green's Harbour was not easy in those days with only dirt roads that were not maintained very well, and no buses or train from our Creston South home. My mother made arrangements with a person that was travelling to St. John's via car. That person picked her up all alone one morning, mother did not go with her. The person she travelled with was not going to Green's Harbour, so she was left at a train station in the small town of Whitbourne, located near a branch road that leads to Green's Harbour. A bad situation for nine-year-old girl to be in. She was dropped by the side of the road with all she owned in the bag she had with her. She had no idea how she was to reach her eventual destination. What sane mother would do this? She was a cruel woman indeed, she really was. My sister stayed around the train station for most of the day feeling alone, with no money, scared, sad and sometimes crying, until a woman talked to her and got her story. She asked where she was going. That woman found a person going to Green's Harbour who would give my sister a drive to her destination. WOW! Imagine a little girl all alone in the middle of nowhere feeling nobody cares about her, could not go back home, no drive back. The only thing possible was to try and go forward. She did reach her destination. Arriving at the place she was supposed to go, she soon realized she was little more than a slave, doing house work and taking care of an old lady — one of the clergy's mother. She says the woman was kind but the husband of the house was not.

One day some months later my father and mother showed up. My father told my sister she could come home but my mother was worried. She said she could come home only if she could take the new clothes she had received with her. My sister did come home then. My father should have left my mother stranded by some road side along the way and never went back; all of us would have been better off. Just writing my sister's story makes me angry. What cruelty!

My other siblings and I received daily beatings from my mother, sometimes it seemed for no reason of all. I remember my sister Elsie bearing the brunt of many vicious beatings whenever mother was in one of her anger tirades.

There was this one time, mother told me she was going to give me away. One late afternoon, there was a strange man — a salesman I think — visiting our house. He was from the capital, and represented big St. John's department stores. He was going door-to-door selling beds and appliances in Newfoundland remote communities, Mother threatened to give me away to him. Did she mean it or plan to for real? I do not know for sure, or was it just a cruel joke. After all, she had tried to give two away already. A child does not know, just feels afraid. I ran out the door terrified, and hid in the forest near our house. I didn't even venture back to get lunch or dinner. I just watched the house from my hiding place until the man left later in the day. Only then did I return home, but I was so fearful that I hardly slept that night.

# CHAPTER SIX

I grew up in out port Newfoundland. If you lived in or were from St. John's NL, you were considered a townie, if from out port NL you were considered a Bayman. The same holds true even today. I was and am a Bayman, born and raised in Mortier Bay/Placentia Bay Newfoundland, I'm a hardy Bay boy indeed, not a Townie. The community where I was born and grew up was divided into Creston South where I grew up, Creston North, and Marystown, accessible to us mostly by row boat only.

My family did not own a vehicle, there were very few cars around and roads were just dirt roads and not very good for driving. They were only good for horse and buggy or walking. When travelling by rowboat we usually did so depending on the tide direction. Going with the tide was easier to travel, the turning of the tide flow determined the direction of travel. When the ocean flow was out, the bay signaled low tide was coming. High tide flow was when the ocean flowed back into the bay. What was important to know was that low tide was usually about 50 minutes later each day. Travel back home by tide flows was easier. It was better and easier not to row against the tide flow. Sometimes I feel like I have been fighting against the tide my whole life.

When I was a boy there was religious segregation — Protestant and Catholic. Not much interaction between the two was accepted. Both Creston South and Creston North were predominantly Protestant, while Marystown was predominantly Catholic. There were lots of religious prejudices at this time in NL history. Unfortunately, religion divided families and friends alike. Creston South had churches such as The Salvation Army, The United Church and The Church of England, Anglican. Creston North had churches such as The Pentecostal and The United churches. A few others have been added today. Marystown had only a Catholic church at this time. Towns divided by religious segregation was common in Newfoundland at the time, a tradition of Irish roots in Newfoundland. I think it is good this tradition has passed. My generation and now the younger generations saw the folly and stupidity of this way of life, and have let go of this foolishness. The generation before did not let it go easy. There was push back from many parents, grandparents, relatives and clergy alike. For me, one religion is not better or more right than another. I just chose what I felt was right for me, as should others. I do not believe in religious segregation or any other type of segregation, for that matter.

Once it was clear that the younger generation had no interest in religious segregation and would marry other religions, even if against parents' wishes, things began to change.

On many occasions parents, grandparents and some other family members and friends refused to attend the wedding of their sons, daughters and friends because they were marrying in a church not of their baptised religion. This was supported and sometimes promoted by their local priest or clergy. Controlling the flock was important. Religious segregation has mostly been let go and gone to a deserved death, although a few may still hang to that or wish that stupidity came back.

Marystown was originally named Mortier Bay, meaning Dead Bay. It was named by the French fishing schooner fleets that moored in the bay to seek shelter from impending storms. The town's name was later changed to Marystown by a parish priest. Apparently, there was no vote on the issue by residents, which is an example of Catholic dominance in Marystown and the power of the Catholic priest.

Clergy in NL have changed over the years, but not without a fight to keep the power and control.

By the time I went to high school, the Protestant religions had integrated in to one school system, named the integrated school system, while the Catholic population held on for dear life only changing just a few short years ago out of financial necessity with dwindling enrollments.

From Kindergarten up to Grade 7, I attended a two-room school house run by the Salvation Army. The teacher was a clergy person, as was common in Newfoundland schools ran by religious segregation (which was all or most schools in this province at the time). There was no religious indoctrination during my school years, but was common in Catholic schools. We had just the Lord's Prayer every morning prior to class start up. Sometimes, we sang the Newfoundland anthem ("Ode to Newfoundland"), the Canadian national anthem ("O Canada"), and, on occasions, "God Save the Queen." The anthems were mostly sung on special occasions but the Lord's Prayer was said every morning. The Lord's Prayer is not said in schools anymore, it has been put to death by Political Correctness. I am and have never been a fan of Political Correctness. Canada was founded on Christian values, so why do we continually try to change that just to pander to immigrants? I do agree with immigration, but why is it that we have to change to accommodate it? Why do we have to say "Happy Holidays", not "Merry Christmas"? Well, I have and will always say "Merry Christmas" and if somebody does not like it, too bad! I think all should be able to pray in their own way. I once read somewhere that Political Correctness is the action of trying to pick up a turd by the clean end. That is a good definition for it, I like it.

Grade school teachers were commonly clergy of a religion who owned and ran the schools. Many Catholic nuns were teachers, and I surmised then that they received pay from the government, not the church. I remember most Catholic kids I knew talked about how mean the nuns were as teachers; they apparently especially liked handing out corporal punishment. This type of punishment was common in most schools run by religious organizations in those times.

In the school I went to there was Kindergarten to Grade 4 in one room, Grade five to eleven in the second room (or "High End", as we referred to it). For school lunches, the richer kids had ham sandwiches and the like. The not so wealthy fisherman kids had lobster, eggs, and chicken sandwiches, and such. How times have changed today.

There was a pot-belly cast iron stove in each school room. This stove burned wood and coal, no electric heat or furnaces. The students were responsible for getting the wood and coal into the school room each morning. The power for lights, the wood and coal, was paid for or supplied by families who had children going to the school not government. We did not have a gym or labs but lots of room to play outside in the school yard. There were two outhouses for toilets: one for boys and one for girls. It is good to note most schools and churches were built by labour and with material provided by the local town folks, not government. When those buildings were sold in later years, the money was hoarded by the churches, not given back to the community. Some buildings may have been sold to pay for court rewards against a church.

For the start of my Grade 8 year, the local Protestant religions changed to an integrated school system which included all local Protestant religious denominations, not any Catholic because they wanted to keep their own system.

During my early school years, I was bullied many times by local bullies. All small towns have those local bullies who eventually grew up to be nothing but assholes and make very little of their lives. There were a few kids of richer folks who grew up sampling drugs. It seems the most popular kids ended up being the least, and some got hooked on the drugs, becoming drug addicts. I think all kids can be assholes sometimes — some bigger than others — even grown up kids.

Other kids, bullies I knew in my childhood, were incarcerated despite having good parents and families.

Not only were bullies mean to me but also some of their parents also. I think this bad treatment of me was mostly because my family received Welfare. Folks receiving welfare was a stigma it seemed. Sometimes bullies were just cheered on by older kids to get some excitement going because they knew this child was poor and did not have much confidences or support. This was not my fault, nor my fathers who had a heart condition, but they were mean none-the-less. Although I left it many years ago. I do not go back often, but as I get older I hear it calling me back. I close my eyes to feel the warm summer ocean breeze again. With closed eyes, I visualize and hear the waves of the ocean and the voices of my younger years. All of this seems to be calling to me, reminding me who I am and from where I came. I believe home is not a place, it is a feeling and I never did and still do not feel at home there. When I do go back there for a visit it is good to see folks from my early years, but most have all gone to start lives elsewhere in Canada and the world. I do feel more at home where I currently live. I have no great memories to draw me back to Marystown, Newfoundland.

I love Newfoundland but my hometown reminds me of not so good times in my life. Marystown was, in my opinion, not a good place to live or for a child to grow up.

My dislike for my hometown is in part, no doubt, due to my childhood years and my experiences growing up living there. I was beaten by my mother, bullied by friends and others, belittled by adults. The biggest sport was gossip: talking about others and interfering in others' business. Gossip is a horrible thing. Making up a story about a person because they heard some details but not all helps people feel important. Gossipers show envy of others doing good, not feeling good for them. They seem to have more glee in people failing then succeeding. It is part of the DNA, it seems.

Humans want to be judge and jury, but judging is not a Godly trait, it is a human trait. John 8:15 says: "You judge according to the flesh; I judge no one"" John 12:47 reads: "As for anyone who hears My words and does not keep them, I do not judge him. For I have not come to judge the world, but to save the world." To me, the Bible seems to say judging is performed by humans not God.

Unemployment Insurance in out port NL became a way of life. Collecting enough weeks to qualify for EI was and is common, but it's a way of life I had no interest in. I left there in 1989 and have not returned very often, and have no interest in living there. I am happy to say I have never collected EI since I left there; I've always worked for a living. I do try to visit Marystown sometimes, but not often.

As a child I did not receive many toys to play with. The school I went to would have a Christmas concert every year. The school kids would prepare for it months in advance. The night would arrive, the school would fill with family, friends and other locals. There was always a Christmas tree and a visit from Santa. Kid's parents would place a present under the tree for Santa to give to their kids. At the end of the concert Santa would arrive with all the audience and all kids on stage singing "For He's a Jolly Good Fellow." Then kids would line up single-file for Santa to hand out the gifts from under the Christmas tree. Santa called each kid whose name was on a gift.

We all were hoping for a present, this happened year after year, but neither my name nor any of the Crocker kid's names were ever called, although we stood waiting in line with the other kids. We were waiting and hoping that maybe this would be the year to get a gift, but we always walked away with tears in our eyes and very disappointed. Other kids had smiles and were happy opening their presents, sharing their joy, showing off their gifts to each other, but never me. As a child, I never understood why Santa never brought a present for me. As a child, I learned to really dislike Christmas and the fact I was born into the Crocker family. Why me? Although I am happy I have so many siblings. I love them all. Even today I do not expect gifts at Christmas. Actually, I'd rather not get any. If one does not expect anything then you cannot be disappointed. Maybe this is the reason why I do not expect a lot out of life although I have worked hard to get ahead and be successful. I have been successful due to my hard work, despite a bad childhood and being raised on social assistance/welfare. Although today I am financially OK, I always feel insecure about possibly not having enough money to last through my ABI and retirement.

At that time, social assistance cheques were not directly deposited into bank accounts (no Internet then). People who had to receive a welfare cheque had to go stand in que at the welfare office once a month. Families had to make the small stipend last for a month, there would be no more. Local town folks would go see who was in line at the welfare office. That news made for good gossip, so it seems. How sad, really

It was not easy for us kids growing up in a family on welfare. There was not much money and there never was any money for kids to have to spend, not even a treat once in a while. As I grow older, those bad memories fade, and forgiveness has become more prominent in my heart, and in my body, mind and soul. I have been able to forgive those many people that did mean and hurtful things to me and my family. My forgiveness is not for them but for my own soul. It feels really great to forgive and I forgive them all. I also pray for God's blessing and forgiveness for them. If Jesus could forgive those that crucified him I think I can forgive all those that chose to hurt me for reasons I do not know or understand. My words to all are: Go in peace and may God bless you with his favour.

# CHAPTER SEVEN

Growing up I had neighbours who were a family by last name of Farewell. Mr. and Mrs. Farewell (Bill and Mini Jane) were angels. Their son, Ray, and I were friends growing up. Many cold winter days when my mother had us locked outside and not allowed back inside to a warm house, Mini Jane would let me inside to play games with her sons. To warm up, she would make us hot milk and such. Both Mini and Bill have since passed and gone to rest in the spirit world as angels I am sure. During the summers, Mr. Bill and Miss Mini took me and many of my brothers and sisters along with their own kids to a restaurant in Burin owned by Miss Mini's sister. They would buy all of us a soft ice cream cone, or a custard cone, as we named it. I think those ice cream cones were the only real treats I ever received during my childhood.

As a kid, I wore a lot of hand-me-downs given by other families. I also wore clothes made over, from bigger clothes of older siblings to make them fit me. Each year, I received only one pair of winter boots and in spring and summer one pair of summer sneakers ("Ball Boots" they referred to them as back then). They were made cheap and were cheap as could be found at the time. My parents did not have enough money to go around, only money enough for absolute necessities and sometimes not even that. We had very little of what we needed and nothing of what we wanted. There were no allowances then for kids to waste hard earned money, is what was said. No treats for kids. I received fresh fruit only at Christmas. Other than that it was fruit picked during summer from local fruit trees. There were no birthday celebrations with a birthday cake or presents. My parents, sad to say, had no interest in celebrating a child's birthday. Birthdays were never celebrated in our house, no birthday party or presents

Even today I do not make a big deal over my birthday. I do not mention it to anybody because there is no need, I always say. Why celebrate getting older? It makes no sense to me. I suppose I could change my thinking about getting older. Now I think getting older should be celebrated. It is good because it means a person is still living — you made it. I suppose parents and kids learned to make the best of what was had and available. My father did work in logging camps until he was diagnosed with a heart condition and unable to work there anymore. My family were then thrown onto welfare after that. Dad hated welfare because he wanted to work. I saw his frustration many times when he got upset, but never did he raise a hand to hit me or my siblings. My father did not have much education, as I remember he or Mother could not read or write. When dad was nine, he was in school one day when his father came to the school house, took him out of school because he had gotten a paying job for him at 5 cents an hour.

Until my family were thrown on welfare and dad could not work anymore due to illness, dad worked at logging and fishing. I remember out of necessity my father became a barber, for a little extra cash. He became a part time barber just to earn a little cash for a few cigarettes and a beer once in a while. He occasionally gave me a nickel to get a treat. He did not have much money other than welfare. The charge for a haircut was 25 cents or he would barter for food, such as fish in place of money. Dad really favoured fish. Deep sea fisherman would come for a haircut during at-home days, which were 2 or 3 days each and 10 days at sea. They brought fish or sea birds, enough for all the family in exchange for a haircut. This was a free meal for a big family (better than money). We ate pan fried fish, fresh and salt fish, fish stew, baked fish, fish cakes, poached fish, fished wrapped in newspaper and roasted in the stove fire, and my most hated meal: cod's head stew! Eat what was cooked or go without we were all told. Going without food sometimes is what happened until the next day at breakfast. It is worth noting that when I was growing up, we had vegetable gardens of cabbage, potatoes, carrots, turnips and beets. We also owned approximately 75 hens just to raise for eggs and meat, not for pets. We also had two horses for pulling wood, not to ride or for pets. There were many chores for boys to do, no idle time because idle hands did the devils work, was said. All the boys were to help cut and store wood for winters, tend summer gardens, take care of horses and cut hay to dry (because wet hay will rot quickly), and collect and take dried hay to the barn for winter storage for feeding our two horses. Young women were expected to help out and did so by doing house chores, which were many, considering a large family in one house with no indoor plumbing. We used a hand pump to fetch water from the spring or well as it was often referred to; we also used buckets sometimes in winter due to freeze ups. Families worked together to get things done. People and families seemed to be much happier than they are today. In winter, the horse slide was hooked to the horse to go into the forest to haul wood. We owned two horses, a chestnut coloured stallion named Jack, and a brown coloured mare named Star. She was named Star because she had the shape of a white star on her forehead. These horses were owned out of necessity to be able to get fire wood for our cold winters. Jack was a strong horse and seemed to have a mind of his own. Usually when we were rigging the horse to get ready for the trip I got to hook the horse belly strap as I was little enough to walk under the horse. I remember dad taking my brother and I on the horse slide, it was fun until we arrived to the wood cutting site. While my father and older brothers cut wood, my brother and I (at age nine and eleven) were expected to tow and pile wood in waist deep snow on a cold winter days. We would get freezing cold and wet. Dad would light a fire to warm and dry us out. We removed our boots that were full of melting snow, our home knitted woolen mittens, woolen hats and woolen socks, and hung them on a branch over the fire to dry. We did not have any snow suits, just long underwear under cotton pants; those stayed on and dried while we sat by the fire, steam flowing from them as they dried from the fire's heat. He also made a lunch or "mug-up" (as it was referred to by many Newfoundlanders at the time) in the woods. Mug-up means lunch in Newfoundland language. It was usually homemade bread with molasses, dried cod fish and a cup of tea steeped in a large juice can. Dad removed the lid and added a piece of wire to allow the can to hang from a makeshift hanger over the fire to boil. Dad also roasted dried fish in the fire. Lunch seemed so tasty, with all of us having a mug-up by the roaring fire. I also did this mug-up in the woods with my son as he was growing up during our many fishing trips to rivers, lakes and ponds. Our horse, the Stallion Jack, seemed to know when it was his last trip out of the forest for the day. On the last slide load of wood for the day, he would not stop at our house to get wood unloaded, even though my father pulled hard on the reins. He would just run on by, heading for the barn. Now I am older I think Jack knew it was his last load of wood because the two smaller fellows were sitting on top of the wood going home for the day or maybe it was the sun was going down for the day. Then, of course, at the barn my father just turned him around and back to our house to unload the wood. After the wood was unloaded my father got Jack and the slide back into the woods to get my two older brothers, who were left to walk home from the wood-cutting area. Back then I thought it was strange that Jack would not stop at the house. Jack was always happy to get to the barn, because there my brother and I had the chore to ensure he was fed with some hay, oats and water for the night. Dad and my older brothers also helped us get it done once they got back to the barn.

Mug-ups were also had in the house of many Newfoundlanders in the late evening prior to bed time, especially if friends were visiting. It was like a lunch prior to heading home for the night. Nobody was allowed to go home without a mug-up. These mug-ups also occurred anytime a person came to visit. There was always a huge kettle at the back of the wood/oil stove with boiled or boiling water and a tea pot with loose tea steeping. The tea was very strong, and tea bags were not available then. A tea strainer to keep tea leaves out of the cup was placed over the cup when pouring tea. The cup was filled to about half with the steeped tea then the boiling water was added to the tea to fill the cup up. Kids usually only got about ¼ cup of steeped tea then it was filled with boiling water. Everyone got tea, there was not any coffee, fruit juice or milk. I am not sure if these items were even available at the time or my parents could not afford to purchase them if they were. Occasionally, a local family that owned a cow or two would drop of a bottle of milk to us. This milk was not drank but turned into cream for making butter. As little boys we were told not to drink coffee because it was not good for you —it shrinks up your penis, ha-ha. There are a lot of superstitions in Newfoundland history, many Newfoundlanders were very superstitious.

Some of them include:

When visiting other homes, it was said you could not leave between 11:55 P.M. and 12:05 A.M. because that was the witching hour. The fairies may take you.

Another common superstition was if you entered a home, later when you left the house you had to always ensure to exit through the same door you came in because if you left through another door you would take all the luck out of the house. It was common to hear people say, "Leave the door you came in."

There was also a superstition if you went into the forest — or as Newfoundlanders say, "into the woods" — make sure your pockets are turned inside-out so the fairies won't get you. Also, take some bread to occasionally drop on the ground to feed the fairies; they like that and will not take you.

Another one is if a broom fell across your doorway that meant there was soon to be a death, so no brooms were ever placed or stored near any door.

Kids spent a lot of time outside playing in my youth. There were no hours inside with video games. We played games such as baseball, ground hockey, soccer, Cowboys and Indians, and we swam in the local ponds and rivers. There were no helicopter parents present. Most boys had a pistol cap gun, but not I, I only used a pistol gun fashioned out of a piece of wood.

Mother I call her — not mom — because she was never a mom. Mom is a woman that encourages a child and makes them feel secure, loved and safe. This woman was not that. Mother was a lot but never a mom. She was an abusive, cruel woman, and would yell, scream, and beat us. We would have many bruises from the beatings. I do not remember Mother or Father attending any school functions like Parent's night, grads or even asking us about school work. Neither of them had very much education. My mother never gave a hug or words of love or encouragement (NEVER), to any of her kids. She really missed out on the joys of being a mother and — as for us kids — we missed out on having a mom, she should have been in jail for child abuse. Her beatings we received happened mostly when dad was not around but if we said anything to dad we would get another beating as soon as he was away from the house. This was used to keep us quiet. I was convinced her intention was to kill us some day.

I remember on cold winter days mother told us to get dressed and she would send us outside and lock door from the inside. We were not allowed back in even when we were crying because of cold and needed to warm up a little. I remember looking in the house window and she would be sitting in her rocking chair drinking a bottle of Pepsi and eating a chocolate bar. These items were always stored away for herself, never shared with us kids. Food in our house was stored in a pantry behind a padlocked door where we kids had no access. Mother had the only key. Later in my life I realized, or sensed, that mother had an untreated mental illness. What else could it be for a woman to be so abusive and cruel to her children? Mental health help was not available like today. Well, I suppose it's not really available today either, unless you can pay $150-$200 an hour for the help. Although governments talk about mental health, it is mostly lip service. In my mother's time even those that asked for help were shunned by others and spoke unkindly about. A common thing others said was that they are "off their head," or "a mental case," or "they need to be in the mental hospital." People were not kind to persons with a mental illness. It seems this has not changed much even today. People with mental illness are still misunderstood and shunned.

My sister, who was just a little girl, was once locked inside a dark room in our house that had no window for a week by Mother. Imagine that: a child locked inside a room in the dark for a week, only given toast for breakfast and whatever was made for supper. If she did not like it she had to go without supper. She cried all day to get out but, no one cared, it seemed. We knew if one of us took pity and tried to let her out we would get the same punishment, so nobody did anything. It was like being locked in a closet really. Imagine the fear and anxiety in a child's mind during that time. WOW. Cruel indeed. When she was released from her prison, the daylight hurt her eyes so much she could not see very well.

My youngest brother, was eventually the only sibling left at home with Mother. Mother did not want him to go anywhere, she was afraid to be alone. Later in Mother's life she eventually married a local fellow who was a widower.

This fellow had his own house but gave it to his son and wife to live in. Soon after, this fellow moved in with Mother and she soon kicked Jason out of the house — told him to leave. He was sleeping in a pup tent just outside his mother's door. Imagine that! At night, she could look out the window and see her youngest son in a nylon pup tent in the yard, but had no compassion for him. I think I was not living in Marystown at this time. We soon also learned it was Mother's decision to kick Jason out of the house, not the new husband. He once commented that he did not know why Violet treated her children so badly. My sister, Lillian, heard about what was happening to Jason. She went to my mother's house, gave her an ear full, took Jason back to her place, and helped him find a job. He eventually moved to Toronto and lived for a while with my sister, Blanch, and family until he got a job and got settled. He then found his own place to stay and moved out on his own. He later married and has been living in Ontario, Canada now for approximately 35 years. He does not return to Newfoundland very often. He also does not have much contact with his siblings. I do not know why he keeps to himself, but has his own reasons I am sure.

Mother was a so-called religious woman and wore the Salvation Army uniform. She was off to church and most times she portrayed herself as a saint. Little did others know maybe they did? It seemed that even when there was not much food around for us there would be lots for strangers and/or friends that came by. Food showed up from nowhere especially when clergy visited. It seems from what I have seen in my life that the so-called religious people are the most abusive.

My father died when I was 13 years old. Dad had attended a wedding and was playing the accordion there and, at the time of his death, my two oldest brothers were sitting on either side of him. The family were getting ready to go on a week vacation the next day to a cabin of my brother-in-law's father. The night before we were to leave to go on a holiday there was a planned outdoor wedding reception for the son of a friend of my parents. I was in Grand Bank, NL, at my sister's house to play soccer for the summer. Her house was across the street from the soccer field in Grand Bank, a Newfoundland outport town. A phone call shortly after midnight woke us up. I remember hearing my sister on the phone and then some crying. I had thought it was something wrong with my brother Frazer.

Apparently, Dad decided not to go to the wedding, but a knock on the door of our family home in Creston South, by people attending the wedding, convinced him to go. So, he brought his accordion with him as usual. He was playing his accordion with my two older brothers, Frazer and Wesley, sitting one on each side of him. My father apparently passed quickly. The rest is sad, as you can imagine. As was the norm in Newfoundland at the time, Dad lay in wake at our family home just across the hall from my bedroom. It was traumatiz-ing for a child, no doubt, but not much attention was given to that at the time. I could see my father's head in the casket as I lay in bed at night; that's scary and sad for a young boy. I still remember it. I remember less and less of my father as time passes, and I find it hard to distinguish between memories and those stories I was told by others over the years. I do remember my youngest sister Beverly having an emotional melt down one night because she could see dad's dead body from her bedroom door while she was in bed at night.

In common Newfoundland character, we tried not to mourn a life too much. We celebrate the life a person had in good Irish fashion: have a drink, play some music, tell stories about them, talk about their life, and celebrate the life lived. The night prior to my father's funeral, many of dad's friends, our relatives and neighbours came to our house and played music in his memory, sang a little, drank some alcohol, talked about my father's life, and some of their experiences with him. Listening to the stories I learned more about my father that night then I had ever known.

After my father died there were seven young children still living at home. It was tough for a young boy. For me, it seems the time in life a boy needs a father the most he was dead. It was probably tough for Mother too.

# CHAPTER EIGHT

Dad being a barber, he always cut my hair. With him not around I did not want a haircut, and I would get it cut when I was ready. I was 19 when I made the decision to cut my hair. As soon as the haircut was finished I was sorry for cutting it. Even today. Using the "Peace" sign, I coined the phrase: "Peace all over your body, man, and let the groove be with you." When I said that, people would answer, "Groovy man, right on." Although I had long hair and portrayed a hippy lifestyle I never did get into drugs of any sort, except to try marijuana a couple times. I did not like it and that was it, I had no further interest in it. I did see lots of it in the 70s. There were a lot of chemical drugs back then, like LSD, Speed and the like. I am thankful I did not use them, but I saw many friends use it.

During my teen years, my hair grew long. From age 13-19 it was very long and thick, down over my back. Now at 60 it is shorter, but thick. Back then I wore bell-bottom jeans and a pair of square, purple lens sunglasses, peace chains around my neck. I was the picture of cool, so I thought. I was a rebel and sometimes I sewed extra material into the bell bottoms to make them bigger.

The common thing in the 70s was hitchhiking everywhere to get around. During the winter of 1971/72 I worked odd jobs to save some money for my trip of a lifetime. I wish I had written each day into a journal on that time. It would make a great book, but I will write a flavour of it here just to give my readers a little knowledge of the trip and my perseverance.

By June of 1972, about three months away from my 16th birthday, I had saved about $200 for my planned trip to hitch hike across Canada from coast to coast to experience my great country the real coast to coast from Newfoundland to Vancouver. As soon as school was out in June of 1972 I set out on my road trip. I was carrying a pack sack that was packed with molasses sandwiches, one pair of jeans, three pairs of underwear, a small nylon pup tent, and a sleeping bag. I was wearing the coolest clothes I had: a pair of patched up, wide bell-bottom jeans, a blue shirt, a jean jacket, a pair of sneakers, and the coolest hat with a multicolored feather stuck in the silk material that was tied around it just above the brim of the hat and I topped the outfit off with a pair of purple coloured, square sunglasses. That first morning when I headed out I felt apprehensive, scared and excited all at once. I was on my way hitchhiking across Canada and back. Leaving in June from Marystown, Newfoundland to Vancouver, British Columbia and then return. I had only read about the places I was going to visit on my way and had very little real knowledge of them. I knew I would have to follow the Trans-Canada highway west to Vancouver. I would visit every province of Canada. There were not any cell phones at this time, but there were pay phones in many locations across the country if I wanted to call home. But why would I want to call home? I just needed to go, get away. From the time I left in June until the time I arrived back home in September, I did not phone home once. I arrived in Vancouver the last week of July. I was elated I had made it. I met a few others there that day performing the same act as me. I arrived back to North Sydney, Nova Scotia, in late September, 1972, with no food — just two aspirins in my pocket and no money to get on the Marine Atlantic Ferry to Newfoundland. I was able to overcome that obstacle with the help of a truck driver. I hid in the sleeping area of his truck behind the front seats until I got on the ferry, then it was ok to get out to roam around. On arriving in Port aux Basques, Newfoundland, I had already hooked up a ride across Newfoundland as far as the very small town of Goobies, which was located at the branch road near the turn off from the Trans-Canada to go down the Burin Peninsula highway to Marystown. I was dropped off at Goobies late one Sunday evening. Now I was approximately a two-hour drive away from where I lived. The next item was to find a ride the remainder of the distance, but it was just starting to get dark. I did get a ride with a fellow going down the Peninsula. We were driving along, then almost to the branch road to the town of Terrenceville. He said he was turning off just up at the Terrenceville junction, and he would drop me there. Terrenceville was about 45 minutes down this branch road and still over an hour's drive to Marystown. There was not a town and there were no street lights. It was dark and foggy with some misty rain by this time. My thoughts were: "What will I to do now?" Here I was, just turned 16, and I was in the middle of nowhere on a dark, foggy, misty night by the side of a road about one third the distance down the Burin Peninsula to Marystown. I had to make a plan fast because I had to get off the road. Other drivers would not see me in the dark, the fog and misty rain, and I could get hit by a car or truck. I got out of his car, found the old flashlight in my back pack and turned it on. The light was really dim because the batteries were just about dead. Getting another ride now was going to be virtually impossible. I found my way off the road shoulder, through a ditch partly filed with water, and onto higher land. I was unable to see very well with the dim light of my flashlight in the rain, drizzle and fog. I went into the low brush next to the road to find a place to make a bed in the low trees that grow really stunted beside the road. I did find a good place in the low growth trees to lay down, because the branches from the trees kept my sleeping bag from touching the wet ground. I got into my sleeping bag and pulled it over my head just as my light batteries went dead. I did not hear any more cars or trucks driving past before I fell asleep. I was really on edge and probably would have crapped my pants at any loud sound, or anything, really. At sunrise, I woke to the sound of a large truck, probably an

18-wheeler. It was off in the distance and the weather had cleared overnight. I quickly gathered my stuff and ran to the roadside to stick out my thumb. I was in luck because the trucker stopped to give me a ride. Arriving in Marystown about two hours later, he dropped me off at the local grocery store where he was to unload his cargo. I then walked the ten miles to where my family house was. I had been travelling and hitch hiking for three months. My hair was longer, I was thinner, I needed a change of clothes and a wash. My mother's first words were "Oh! You are home. Are you?" That was all she said, nothing else. I made myself some toast and tea, and took a sponge bath. Our house did not have a shower or any indoor toilet yet. I then went to bed. I was beat. I fell asleep thinking about my road trip, and was happy about my great experience. It's an experience that has meant more to me as I got older. I will never forget that summer. In today's world, a missing person's report would be filed on behalf of helicopter parents. They do not understand the necessity of a young son or daughter getting out on their own to explore themselves and the world around them. They do not understand the need of their children to learn from their own experiences and mistakes, not their parent's mistakes and experiences. You do not know or understand what you do not experience or feel. If you tell a small child something is hot, they have no idea what you are talking about until they touch something it and feel it for the first time. It's an experience they do not soon forget. After touching a hot surface they now know what hot really is because they have experienced it. In present days, parents do not want their kids to have their own great experiences. They do not want to send their kids to school without a cell phone, just in case. I do understand the world today is a lot less safe than in my teen years. Hitchhiking is not a recommended or safe way of travel for any teens today. Try not to let fear run your life.

The only way my parents got a message to me when I was a kid outside playing with my friends, was to go outside and ask people if they saw me anywhere or tell others that — if they saw me — to tell me they were looking for me, and I should come home. One time, a gentleman, walking by where I was playing ground hockey with my friends yelled to me, "George, your mother is looking for you, best for you to go home." ASAP. Sometimes it takes a village to raise a child. The insecurity bestowed on kids today by parents and TV news is just unbelievable. Sometimes kids will fall down, and that is ok. Parents just need to ensure their children have a safe place to fall. They will get back up on their own, just give them a chance, just believe in them and the knowledge you have raised a good child. Like a bird with babies in her nest, understand your job is to teach them to fly on their own, then let them go. Let them soar to their own heights, and cheer them on.

That summer on the road were the best and probably most important months of my lifetime. I felt free, just travelling across my beautiful big country of Canada, meeting some great people like me. Occasionally, I took a side trip away from the Trans-Canada Highway. I was given a ride in Alberta by a group of long haired friends of Jesus in a Volkswagen micro bus. That ride was truly amazing and "groovy."

Another time I set up my pup tent in what seemed like a tent city near Saskatoon. People like me were just hanging out at camp fires, smoking dope, drinking beer. If you did not have any it did not matter, what was available was shared around by those who had it. The attitude was: everybody shared what they had. Young teenagers, none over 20 it seemed, living in tents, travelling and exploring their country of Canada, sitting around campfires playing guitars and singing songs together. It was an amazing night. A groovy time indeed.

I always thought I was anti-establishment, so to speak, but was I really? I laugh about it today when I tell my kids and others, but think about a time in history that truly was amazing. I am happy to have lived in and experienced the 1970s, and I wish my kids were so lucky. I do thank my mother for allowing me to experience, enjoy and really live, that time of my life, letting me fly on my own. I really soared like an eagle.

In the summer of 1973, after high school graduation, I got my first job working at a Gulf gas station. I got paid $1.58 per hour, and paid rent to mother. "Nobody stays for free when working," she said. I made about $58 a week, about $50 take home. I had to pay mother $15 a week, and that probably did me some good because I guess I was learning responsibility. At the age of 17, I was forced out of the house where I grew up. Mother did not want me around anymore and kicked me out on the street to fend for myself. I was only a kid really, but I found a way to survive as best I could. This was the start of the next phase of my life. On my own at 17, one could not imagine this in today's world, but in the 1970s in my hometown, kids were expected to grow up, get a job and go out on their own, not stay home and be taken care of by their parents. Besides, I think Mother just wanted me gone and not around for her to deal with.

I have been working and providing for myself, and eventually a family, since then. Nobody to call for help or to go for help even if it was necessary.

# CHAPTER NINE

With 15 in my family there were always people around; that is just the way it was. Not much room for others but, it seemed always room for more.

A sad day in my life was the day my brother, Fraser, was killed. I was 16 at the time. He shared a bedroom with my brother Freeman and me, until he got married to Linda. Fraser was 25 years old at the time of his death in 1972. He had been working on his car, had it sitting on wooden blocks to work underneath it when the car slipped from the blocks, falling onto him. The family was devastated by this loss. His pregnant wife and a two-year-old son, plus mother, father, and brothers and sisters were left to mourn this great loss. I remember his heartbroken son looking under beds trying to find his dad, calling out to a dad that he would never see again — at least not in living human form. So sad. Today that little boy, Michael, is a spiritual, wonderful grown man with a family of his own, a wife and daughter. He is a great husband and father. Fraser's pregnant wife later gave birth to a healthy baby girl, who today has her own family, a husband and a child of her own. She is a wonderful wife and mother.

As I grew older I did not remember the location of Fraser's grave, but did remember the cemetery location. I had thought about going to visit it, and I would ask mother about it, but all she would say was, "I do not remember where it is either but he is buried near Linda's father, Mr. Corbin." He should have been buried in Creston South near his own father. So, on a visit to Newfoundland some years ago I decided to go look in the cemetery where he was buried, to visit him and bring some flowers. When I arrived at the Salvation Army cemetery in Burin Bay, to my dismay the place had almost grown over with many alder trees, and other shrubs and bushes. I could not find his grave. After all, I was only 16 when he was buried in the middle of a Newfoundland winter with lots of snow on the ground. His wife, or anyone else it seemed, had never visited the grave site to mark it or upkeep it. This all left me feeling sad and dismayed. I left the cemetery saying a prayer for my brother. I said, "Fraser, my brother, I could not find your grave but I know that you know I am here. I know you have found peace and happiness with God and we will met again in that after life." As I spoke, a butterfly settled on a flower in front of me, it did not move as I bent down to see it. It just stayed settled on the flower as if to say, "Yes, I am here and I know you are also." I later spoke to my siblings about the state of the cemetery, then a couple of years later, my brothers Wesley and I went there to visit because we were told Fraser's son decided to find the grave and mark it. We found the grave this time and it was well marked and kept in good condition, unlike the cemetery. We said a prayer at the grave site, feeling sad once again about the loss. Many cemeteries in Newfoundland located in many small Newfoundland towns are in disarray because family members have moved elsewhere to live, or have died and now Mother Nature is reclaiming her ground. These cemeteries are not well kept by the churches that own them, nor by family members that no longer are around the areas. It's sad to say, but in many cases the churches have closed the doors in those locations, due to lack of parishioners and money. In some cases, the community itself no longer exists. The residents have relocated elsewhere. Resettlement has happened to many Newfoundland out port towns, especially as the town's population grew older and all the young people left for other places and bigger centre. There are many stories about Newfoundland resettlement. I will not tell them here because I would not be able to do justice to them.

# CHAPTER TEN

When I was a little boy I did not have a sleigh for sliding on the snow covered hills of Crocker's lane, but all my friends did. Most were store-brought sleighs. A man who lived just down at the end of Crocker's lane made a sleigh for me. He called me inside one day and gave it to me. I noticed it did not have shoes on its runners to help it go fast and said so. Shoes were usually a thin strip of metal such as tin attached at bottom of the runners that allowed the sleigh to glide better/faster over the hard-packed snow. This old man, Mr. Tom Rogers, agreed but said he only had a piece of tin stove pipe available to use. With that, he cut two strips of tin from his stove pipe and added them to my new sleigh. Now, one should be aware there was not much money in those days. A good piece of stove pipe was considered costly and hard to acquire because it had to be ordered in Burin and handmade by a tin smith at a location probably a half days' walk away, or hours by horse and cart. There were very few automobiles available then, so driving or getting a ride was very unlikely. I was happy indeed. This act of kindness by this old man has never been forgotten by me or others in my family. People did not have money available, even small amounts back then. What little they had was to buy only things they needed. There was never money for wants, so cutting up a stove pipe for a sleigh was a very charitable and kind thing to do. I had many hours of fun using that sleigh. In a way, it changed my life for the better.

I was run over by a horse slide full of teenagers sliding one winter evening after dark on a moonlit night. I was sliding on the snow-covered hill of Crocker's lane with my friends and siblings. A horse sleigh was a big sleigh used for horses to pull wood. Medicine was primitive around my hometown back then, but doctors did a great job of patching me up. I spent many months in a primitive and not very well equipped Burin Cottage Hospital. My legs were placed in traction, as was common in those days for broken bones. It was hard on a kid, but necessary I suppose. It was early spring when I got out of hospital. Wade, my best friend, was the first person at our door wanting me to come out to play, even though I had cast on my legs and not able to walk yet. Unfortunately, I have to write that Wade died of an aneurism a few years ago. It is a loss I felt intensely. He was a good guy but had some issues no one was aware of. After release from hospital with the broken leg, I learned we had a TV. It was purchased by my oldest brother after he got his first paying job. It was only the second TV in our town, and it brought kids and adults alike to our house to watch in black and white (no colour TV yet). It seemed people were always around and this TV brought a lot of death to our house. Prior to TV in Newfoundland there was a great art of storytelling, music and dancing during evenings after supper and into the night. Storytelling by parents, grandparents, aunts, uncles and visitors alike was common. My father and Grandmother Crocker played music — the accordion — some evenings while people danced. With the addition of TV these wonderful evenings all soon faded and died a tragic death. I still remember parts of the many stories I heard during those evenings before television came. I have fond memories of my father and grandmother playing music. Soon, we all just sat and stared at a TV screen. I remember parents and visitors watching such programs as "Gunsmoke," "The Red Skelton Hour," "Bonanza," "The Ed Sullivan Show," "Tarzan," "Branded," "The Man From U.N.C.L.E," "The Virginian" and, of course, on Saturday evenings "Hockey Night in Canada" with Foster Hewitt calling the play-by-play. As more and more TVs arrived in our neighbours' houses, these TVs soon ate my boyhood friends also.

At home laid up with a broken leg I still completed my school books with my sister's help, and also completed end of year exams. They were administered by my teacher at my house while I was at home lying on my back with my right leg in a plaster cast, my left leg in a plaster cast down to my knee. This plaster cast covered my thighs and continued up to my belly button. The cast had a small area cut in the front for urinating and an area at the rear to allow using the bathroom facilities or bed pan for bowel movements. There was a plaster brace between my legs to restrict movement. It was difficult for a kid indeed but I did pass exams to go forward to the next grade. I was really lucky not to miss a full school year. It's one of the many times in my life that I needed inner strength to persevere.

During my broken leg recovery, my father carried me around to get me where I needed to go. I do not remember much about the role my mother played back then, and I am not sure why. I did not have a wheelchair then either maybe due to lack of finances for my family. About mid-summer most of the plaster cast was removed, and I got a pair of homemade crutches: two broom handles cut to fit with a short piece attached across the top for under my arms. I did not complain, I had some freedom finally. Before summer was over I was free of all plaster casts, back playing again and ready to return to school. I learned early in life not to give up, and the meaning of perseverance and grit. Little did I know this trait would serve me well me in years to come.

It seems I did get my share of ailments and accidents. One time my foot was severely cut by a piece of glass while swimming. Somebody had thrown a broken Coke bottle into the swimming hole we frequented. I was not taken to a doctor to get it stitched up, or given any type of doctor's medical care. I got iodine and some type of ointment spread on it. This hurt like hell but it sterilized it I was told. And no crying was necessary: boys do not cry. I still have the scar on my foot to show for it. I would pull on my sneakers over the foot and hobble around with the help of two broom or mop handles cut to fit under my arms and a piece of wood nailed across the top. They were make shift crutches and my foot was sore all summer. I hobbled around but it did heal eventually in time for back to school.

Another time I was helping to take apart an old barn for firewood and I drove a rusty nail into the bottom of my foot. No doctor this time either, no need it was said. Mother or grandmother prepared and placed a hot bread poultice on my foot, wrapping it tight with a clean rag. The poultice was to draw out any poison. My foot was sore for days, and a new, clean poultice was placed on it daily. These were commonly used for home remedies in the 1960s in Newfoundland.

What is a poultice? It is made by mashing herbs, plant material or another substance with warm water or natural oils to make a paste. The paste can be applied directly to the skin and covered with a piece of clean cloth. If the herb used is potent, such as onion, garlic, ginger, mustard, etc., you may want a layer of thin cloth between the skin and the the herb. The cloth can then be covered with plastic wrap to hold in the moisture. The poultice can be changed every 3 to 4 hours or whenever it dries out. A compress is used the same way but usually warm liquids are applied to the cloth instead of raw substances. Tinctures or herbal infusions are great for compresses.

I noticed each time the bandage was changed that the poultice had a dark spot, showing it was withdrawing the poison (or so my mother said). Anyway, it did work and soon I was back being an active kid. I heard many times that people do not go to doctors unless necessary. Even today, I think the same way. I do not go to a doctor unless I think it is absolutely necessary — some say I am too stubborn to go. I am sure there are and have been times I needed to or should go but did not, maybe because I thought it was better to be strong and fight it. It is important to be strong, I was taught.

# CHAPTER ELEVEN

At about 16 I was hoping to find a girl to hang around with. After all, I thought I was a cool dude, with long hair down my back, wearing bell-bottom jeans with some cool patches. I had purchased the jeans myself with money I earned collecting beer and pop bottles along the road side between Creston South and Burin. I usually returned the bottles to a local hangout for cash, usually 2 or 3 cents each for pop bottles, and 30 cents for a dozen beer bottles (if the bottles were in the beer case). Most Saturday mornings from early spring to late fall Freeman and I visited the local dump site at a place named Black Brook to find bottles, checking the roadside for empties as we walked. During the winter and occasionally in spring and summer, I would get asked by a local shopkeeper to stack products on store shelves, and in their small warehouse. On Saturday mornings, I would get two or three dollars for working four to five hours, and I was happy to get it. There were no allowances given to kids in those days, and no complaining of not being paid enough for work done. If you wanted money then you were expected to find a way to earn it, not be given it for no reason. One summer, I spent most weekdays digging out under a local fellow's house to allow him to make a basement. I used a pick, shovel and a wheelbarrow to carry the dirt outside to pile in another location I usually got paid about two or three dollars a day. One Friday night in mid-spring 1972, I found a girlfriend while attending a teen dance at a local Catholic-owned community centre named Saint Gabriella's Hall. The dance was organized and ran by a Catholic Church teen committee in Marystown. Well, I did not have the $1.25 required for admission, so a few friends and I pooled our money to make up the amount. The plan was I would pay to get inside, then during the dance I was to go to the bathroom and open the window located at the back of the building that was not lit from the outside. I would let the others in through the window, then immediately after the band break, all would come out of the bathroom with other teens, and nobody would notice. This worked for us time and time again. It was at these dances that I met Sharon, my now ex-wife, mother of our two children, and grandmother to our granddaughter. Sharon attended high school at the Marystown Central High, a Catholic school, while I attended Pearce Regional High — a high school in the integrated, non-denominational system. She was a year or so older than me, but she became my high school sweetheart. She invited me to escort her to her Prom later that same year, and I gladly accepted and attended. I met her parents at the same time. Sharon's mom was a really nice woman, and I could tell Sharon was so much loved by her. I graduated in 1973 and Sharon attend my Prom with me. My parents did not attend my graduation — I was not expecting them to, but hid my disappointment.

I remember Sharon had such beautiful, curly red hair, a great smile, and I thought she was a good dancer and good looking. Of course a young man is thinking mostly with his raging hormones. Sharon I were soon going steady.

Sharon grew up with a very caring, loving mom who died of kidney failure in August 1973. She was 43 years old, and left behind eight kids still living at home. There were five daughters and three sons, plus four sons married and living on their own. Sharon was the oldest daughter at 17 and was still living at home. Her sister, Imelda, was next oldest and still living at home. Maude's death was hard on the entire family. Tom would have to raise the kids alone, with help from his older two daughters. Sharon and Imelda took on the role of mother, and I think Sharon never let that role go as the remainder of the kids grew up. Most of those young children are now married with their own families.

In 2016 Sharons brother Fabian died at age 50 of an apparent heart attack — a sad day for all. I awoke in the middle of the night to hear him talking to me.

"I have been trying to find the crowd," he said (which I assumed meant his siblings).

"Fabian," I said, "I cannot see you."

"Reach out your hand, touch me on the back, then you will see me," he said.

I reached out and could see him very well and was not scared. He had a very surreal, white, peaceful light surrounding him.

"I went to my own house but nobody was there, so then I went to the old man's [his father's place] but the house and all the crowd are gone now. But the old man was still in the meadow," he said.

That was kind of weird because Tom died in the 1980's.

"You're the only one I could find," he said.

I explained that the old house belonging to his father had been torn down some time ago and all his brothers and sisters were all living in other places. The next morning I got a phone call from Suzanne telling me Fabian had died the previous day. His death was very upsetting to me and all his family. He was cremated wearing his Toronto Maple Leafs jersey, his favourite hockey team since anybody can remember.

# CHAPTER TWELVE

I was 18 in 1974 and, with few options for my future, I applied for and was accepted to a college in St. John's NL, about a four-hour drive from my hometown. I was accepted under a Canada Manpower (Service Canada) program that paid for school as well as offering me $60 a week for accommodation and personal expenses. There was no help from Mother or anybody else. Off I went to St. John's for nine months to college, hitching a ride with a few fellows going for the same reason. The first thing to do was find a place to stay in the city, which I did. It was not very good accommodation, but it was what I could afford. I walked the four miles to college and back every day in the fall, winter and spring. I eventually graduated in June 1975, with no family present. Just before graduation I applied for and was offered a job at the Halifax, Nova Scotia shipyard if I graduated. I did graduate and accepted the job. I graduated on a Friday night, then boarded a plane Saturday afternoon destined for Halifax. I had never been on a plane before but the flight went well. My plan was to hopefully start work on Monday morning or as soon as possible.

I moved to Halifax, Nova Scotia in 1975 with my girlfriend, Sharon. My sister was already living in the area, so I made arrangements to stay with her and her husband, paying them some rent, of course. We were grateful to my sister and husband for opening their home to us for two months or so, as she had agreed to allow us to board with her while saving some money that would allow us to live on our own. I soon learned my sister was not an easy woman to live with because she had severe Obsessive Compulsive Disorder (OCD).

Sharon also soon found a job in Halifax. Her brother was a member of the Navy so he was based in Halifax also but was at sea most of the time.

After getting work and earning and saving some money we later found and moved into our own apartment in early September 1975. We did not have furniture, appliances or dishes. Those items were our next on the to-do list. We went to Sears' bargain basement to shop for items of necessity to run a home, gradually buying the things we needed with cash (not credit cards). I am not sure if anybody shopped with credit cards in those days. Folks mostly used cash except for big furniture items from a furniture store. Our first furniture grouping was a three-room bedroom set, couch with coffee and end tables, and a chrome table set. We also purchased a carpet roll for the living room. I remember it cost us $1500 and was on credit for one year. We did not have that amount of money, but we did get it paid off in six months instead of the year that we had. Working hard we acquired the items we needed to be more comfortable than we had ever been in our lives. Soon a decision was made for the next step: get married. Plans were made for the wedding to take place on November 29, 1975. It was a marriage that would last for more than 20 years and bare two great children, a son and a daughter. I recall it was also a happy time for us, our own place, working, making money, living well. We were in love, all was good with the world it seemed. Those are the real golden years.

Sharon soon was feeling ill. She visited doctors and eventually was kept in hospital because she was diagnosed with TB of the kidneys. Doctors said they could treat and cure this disease but it was a serious condition. She started treatment at the hospital and later took treatment at home most of the time. While Sharon was in hospital, I decided to buy a car. It is not the best decision I ever made, and I had to go to driving school for training. It was a 1976 Pontiac Acadian hatchback. It was $3600, a large sum in those days. After release from hospital, Sharon soon lost her job, we thought because of her illness. Not a lot could be done about it then. Sharon and I soldiered on and survived just fine. We had no help from anybody and there was nobody to ask for help from, really. Asking for help would be admitting defeat. We were not defeated and had no quit in us. We learned to survive and take care of ourselves at a young age. We knew we would do fine because we were hardy, proud Newfoundlanders!

For reasons I do not know, I remember on a visit back to Newfoundland I went to a local mall in Marystown. There I noticed an older gentleman who had been a friend of my father's. On approaching him, I introduced myself, he remembered me. He said I look like my father. I thanked him and asked what his secret for staying so young looking.

"I am 88 years old," he said. "I walk every day, it is good for me. All my friends got married, they are all dead. I never did get married, I am still here.

"You could be right. Most divorced men do say that also," I said with a laugh as I walked away.

# CHAPTER THIRTEEN

I lost my job. I was laid-off at the Halifax shipyard in September 1976. Sharon wanted to move back to NL to help her father raise her siblings. So, back to Newfoundland we went and moved in with her father. Living there was good for her helping out her younger siblings, but her father, Tom drank a lot of beer. When sober he was the best man anyone could imagine but give him a drink and the meanness soon came out. By the spring of 1977, we could not handle living with Tom anymore, so we decided to find our own place. Soon after moving away from Tom, we decided it would be great to start our own family. In 1978, Sharon and I discussed and decided we would like to have our own home before our first child was born. For our wedding, Tom had given us a building lot of land in the Basin, located at Marystown North, where his family (the Mitchells') had owned land for generations.

We decided to build a house as soon as possible and informed Tom of our decision. He then decided he wanted to be paid for the land he had given us for a wedding present. He wanted the money before he would sign the papers to change over the deed and the land ownership.

We were busy trying to find work. I completed an application to the Marystown Shipyard and was hired in July 1977 on a recommendation from the steel trade Superintendent, Heber Pike. I am grateful to him to this day. I continued working as a tradesman at the shipyard full time from 1977 until I was laid-off in1989. I was laid off a few times in between for short term intervals. It gave us a real chance at life. We had our own land and a job to build our house, we were happy. Our house build started in the summer of 1978. I cleared and prepared the land using a chain saw and muscle. We acquired a mortgage from CMHC, and planned to build a house measuring 26 X 45 feet. The house would eventually cost us $28,000. It is not a significant sum today, but it was a lot of money then considering my wage was $3.75 per hour. We wanted move into our own place for Christmas 1978. Stefan, our son, was to be born in April 1979 but was born in early March — a few weeks premature. We were so happy to be able to bring him home to our own home, his own home. We knew the importance of having a home not a house. I believe readers know there is a huge difference between a house and a home.

After Stefan was born, Sharon and I decided we wanted two children, hopefully a boy and a girl. So within a few years Sharon was pregnant again. In July 1982, our beautiful daughter Suzanne was born. We were so proud and happy to have a son and a daughter. Life was moving in the right direction it seemed.

While Sharon was pregnant with Suzanne we were told the results of testing revealed the child's head was enlarged and would probably be born "retarded." They did not say mentally handicapped — there was no Political Correctness then. This was not good news for young parents to be. It was very worrisome indeed. I went home and said to young Stefan that he and I had to go somewhere. We drove to Marymount, the little sanctuary in Marystown where a large statue of the Virgin Mary the Madonna resides. This place is located on a dirt road, referred to as Tolt Road. The road is not well kept — it is full of pot holes and ruts, and it's best to drive on it with an SUV. Just three or four km on this road and you would notice Marymount, just off to the left. The entrance road is short but very rough to drive on. At the top of the hill is an approximately 15-meter statue of the Madonna with a prayer sanctuary that is surrounded by a chain link fence and a gate that is never locked. From this point, you can see most of Marystown. To the right one can view most of Mortier Bay, the small town of Spanish Room, and the narrows of Creston Inlet and Birchy Island; it is a spectacular view. Birchy Island was originally owned by the Cleal family, the first settlers of Creston South. It has been passed down through generations and some members of that family still own it I am told. The first Cleal came from England settling on the island and surviving through farming and fishing. Looking to the left about 15 km up Creston Inlet there is a point where it has a Y. To the left of this Y, the narrow inlet opens up into a wider area known locally as the Sou West. With binoculars, one can see marshes, some low-lying trees and the fresh water lake or pond, as locals refer to it, just beyond the shores of the salt water. Most inland water areas in Newfoundland are not referred to as lakes but ponds. Although not visible, there is a river that empties into the fresh pond called Main Brook. This brook also empties out of the pond and runs to the salt water area that is referred to as the Sou West. There are a few very small islands scattered around the Sou West. Looking slightly right in the other direction at the Y of Creston inlet, it continues along to an area known locally as The Nor West. Creston Inlet was and is a great place for boating and water sports in summer. As a young boy, we would go row boating in dories with oars that were long and heavy, requiring one young boy for each oar. Also used here were motor boats built by local boat builders. Today the sheltered inlet is used for mostly boats, sea-doos and water skiing, by locals and visitors alike.

As I understand it, the Madonna statue was erected as requested by a resident of Marystown who had moved to Montreal many years before. He died and in his will made money and land available to erect this statue and prayer garden.

That day I drove there to pray and ask for a miracle, a favour from the Madonna the Virgin Mary. Upon arriving I took a deep breath and scanned my eyes across the beautiful view. Stefan and I kneeled to pray. Stefan started his prayer: God bless mommy and daddy, God bless Stefan, make him a good boy etc. It was the prayer we taught to him at night just before bedtime. I smiled but did not interrupt him. I knew Mother Mary was aware of the reason for our prayers. I prayed to the Madonna and her son Jesus explaining the possibility of my daughter being born with an enlarged head and possibly being mentally handicapped or worse. I remember explaining to Mary that she was a mother and understood our concern. I asked her to intercede on our behalf and asked that she would ensure our child would be born normal as could be.

Suzanne was born a few months later, a few weeks premature. Late one evening Sharon went into premature labour, and I rushed her to the local hospital in my car. She was soon diagnosed as being in labour and the baby was in breach position so could not be born this way. In an emergency situation Sharon, along with an emergency incubator, was transferred by ambulance from the Burin Hospital to the Grace Maternity Hospital in St. John's NL. Later that night after dropping Stefan at his Grandfather Mitchell's house, I drove to St John's to be with her. Sharon's brother accompanied me on the drive. I remember about half hour from Marystown I noticed in the rush I had forgotten to get gas. I had to stop but I did not have any cash. We did not have a credit card either, but the gas station owner said no problem fill it up, drop by and pay on your way home. In today's world that kindness would not happen. I filled the car and continued on my way. I did return to pay with money and gratitude, on my way home some days later. The next day I was informed that, due to pregnancy complications, Sharon had to have a C-section, and it would be scheduled for the next morning. Doctors informed us that the surgery had to be performed to save baby and mother. It was worrisome and stressful, indeed. Lots of prayers went to the heavens that night, prayers for Sharon and baby, said by me, other family and friends.

Before going in to surgery, Sharon said to me, if you are not here when I wake up I will know things did not go well with the baby. The nurses brought the baby out after her delivery. We had a baby girl and she was absolutely perfect, her head was perfectly formed as was the rest of her tiny body. She did not have any so-called defects of any kind. Thank you Mother Mary I prayed immediately. I believe my prayers at Mary Mount were answered a miracle was my first thoughts, and then I phoned Sharon's father. Stefan was with him and I announced the great news. Stefan's first words about it to me on the phone were: "But Dad, I don't want a sister, I want a baby brother."

"Stefan, I think Mom and Dad are happy she is here and healthy," I said.

Today he says he is so happy to have Suzanne for his sister. I soon left the hospital to buy some clothes for her to wear. Back then we were not able to know the sex of the baby before it was born, so I was off to the local stores do some shopping. I drove to K-Mart, the closest department store near the hospital. I bought a set including a pink sweater, a hat, a dress, and a pink blanket and pyjamas as small as I could find. While I was gone shopping, Sharon had woken up and feared the worst. When I arrived back to the hospital I informed her of all the happenings. I should have stayed there at the hospital for sure but thought I was doing the right thing at the time. Today that little girl is Suzanne, who is 35 and a beautiful young woman and mother. She has a little girl of her own and she serves our country as a member of our Canadian military. She was recently promoted to the rank of Master Corporal. My little soldier, a member of The Canadian Air Force. She still has the pink blanket I purchased for her the day she was born. She has taken this blanket with her wherever she travels, always keeping it safe from harm. She used it as she sucked her thumb and snuggle blanket until she grew out of her teens. She still has it, but does not use it as a suck her thumb snuggle blanket anymore. Although the thumb sucking has stopped it is a little ragged now, but not bad considering the years and the wear and usage it has received. Suzanne really is a miracle of the Madonna, the Virgin Mary of Marymount in Marystown Newfoundland. Although I did not know it at the time, this would not be my only miracle; I too would one day be a walking miracle myself. Today Suzanne has her own little miracle her daughter my granddaughter Charlotte who has her own pink blanket that I gave her when she was born. She has named her blanket "Peep," maybe because I would cover her head with it then pull it away uncovering her eyes slowly saying "peep" to get her to laugh or smile. She is now four years old and a joy indeed.

Sometimes, day-to-day life was a struggle raising two kids on one income. Sharon also worked for a salary when work was available. She was never a lazy woman, she always worked hard. We made a home and a good life, for us and our children.

In 1982, Pope John Paul II visited St. John's. My family and I were chosen from the local Catholic Church to be one of the families to be at the airport to bid good-bye to the pope as he left to go visit other places in Canada. It was raining hard the morning of his departure, but Stefan and I were lucky to get a personal blessing from Pope John Paul II. That meeting and blessing changed my life, and I soon decided I wanted to become a Catholic. I was never baptised, but I was christened (referred to as "dedicated" in the Salvation Army religion). The Salvation Army religion does not baptise children. Later in life this became a concern of mine, especially after my kids were born. I queried the Salvation Army minister at the time about the possibility of baptism for each child, but the answer was we do not do that. At that, Sharon and I decided to baptise them at the Catholic Church. Both of us strongly believed baptism was necessary, per bible teachings. Sharon was Catholic. Although we married in the Salvation Army Church in Halifax, NS, Sharon stayed true to her religion over the years. After the Pope's visit, I decide I wanted to be baptised and did so at the Catholic Church in Marystown. It was my decision alone and I have never regretted it. I have questioned my faith in Catholic Church when all the sexual abuse allegations came out. After Pope John Paul II's death and his replacement by Pope Benedict, I refused to go to church until he was gone. It was my opinion that he was one of the problems from the beginning, even before he was Pope. When he retired, the current Pontiff, Pope Francis, came along and he is a pope I can support. Soon after Francis was proclaimed, I started attending church again.

Sometimes, I am not sure I am Catholic enough to be Catholic. I really dislike the fact that the church covered up all the sexual abuse of young boys by priests. It was hard to forgive them for that and, even today, I think it is the main reason why the number of practising Catholics in North America is dwindling constantly. It is a dying religion in the Western world, probably due to all the child abuse scandals.

At one time, Sharon and I were having some marriage issues. One evening after an argument, I went to Mother's place and asked if it was ok to stay there that night. Her immediate answer was "No, indeed." Imagine that: refused a place to sleep by Mother twice in one lifetime. I found a place out of sight to park and slept in my car that night.

One evening, Sharon told me she noticed I did not hug the kids or praise them much. "Do you know how to love them?" she asked.

I thought about that for a time and it caused a light to switch on in my brain. I was repeating what I had learned as a child from my own mother. I did not know how to love my kids because I had not been shown how to love or received any love or kind words from my own mother. I decided to change that pattern immediately, and from that day forward I hugged my kids often and told them how much they were loved. I showed them and spoke kind, loving words to them whenever the occasion was needed. I continue this today. Sometimes for no reason in particular I praise them and tell them they are loved. I thank Sharon for pointing out to me what I was doing because it changed my life and my kids' lives for sure.

Sharon and I filed for separation in 1999. It was time because our marriage had run its course. By 2003, we were divorced. I will not write about the reasons why. Every marriage that breaks up has two stories, that of the husband and that of the wife. Both believe their version is correct because they see it from their own point of view, but in the end, none of that matters. It is lost, it is over, and both lives go on. The important thing is to never put your children in the middle of a divorce if you really love them because they do not deserve that. Be bigger than the hurt in your heart and put them first every time. Feed the dog of love not the dog of vengeance and hate. Before the divorce was finalized Sharon met a fellow in the office she was working at in Halifax. They moved in together and after divorce was finalized she got married. Dave seems to be a great fellow, who has a daughter and grandchildren of his own. When I see Sharon now it seems to me she was just a woman I once knew. I have no feelings about her of any kind and I have completely let go of that chapter of my life. I just feel happy for her and Dave, and I wish them well.

**Marymount located in Marystown Newfoundland**

# CHAPTER FOURTEEN

Stefan soon became a favourite of Grandfather Tom, who came to visit him often. On many occasions, he took him to his house where he spoiled him a little. Tom had stopped drinking at this time in his life.

Tom had a pantry where there were cupboards for dishes and food. The opening to this area had no door but just a wooden door frame. I went to Tom's place one day to pick up Stefan and noticed Stefan was using a hammer to drive nails into the pantry wood door frame. I told him to stop it, but Tom said that it was ok. "There is lots of wood to buy to replace it. No big deal!" Stefan spent many hours at his grandfather's house driving nails into the wooden door frame. Being encouraged by his grandfather of course. Tom replaced the wooden door frame often, and brought Stefan more nails to pound into that wood. This continued over and over again, replacing the wood and buying more nails. Tom also taught Stefan to skate on the ice of the frozen salt water bay out back of his house. He was making figure eights, grandfather would say. Tom also on occasion accompanied me to the local ice rink for general skating. While there, he spent time with Stefan encouraging his skating abilities. In later years, I coached minor hockey and noted that Stefan was always one of my best skaters. Unfortunately, his puck-carrying ability was lacking.

This one time, I went to Tom's house and noticed Stefan had a spoon in his hand and was getting something out of the cupboard. I yelled at him to get out of there. Stefan turned, looked at me, and said, "Dad, my pop is the boss of this house." I almost burst out laughing but had to conceal it because kids need to respect their parent's voice and request. Tom, who was nearby, said to Stefan, "I told you it was OK but if your father says it is not ok then Dad is the boss."

"Well, if your pop said it was ok, then it is ok," I said.

With a big smile, Stefan turned his attention back to the cupboard to get the jar of peanut butter.

On many of Tom's visits to our house, he would say to Stefan, "lets go to dark Tickle to fix the moon." Tom would take Stefan halfway down the basement steps and turn out the lights. We could hear them having a great chat. Tom knew that without lights, a child's mind would open up and have great wonderment. On another visit, Tom went into Stefan's room with him. We could hear Tom encouraging him to do something but was not aware of what it was. We could hear him say that Stefan was so good, and was a smart boy. Sharon went into the room later after they had come out. I heard her start to lose it. Apparently, Stefan had marked up the walls of his room up as high as he could reach with Crayon. Of course, encouraged by his grandfather. Tom said that Stefan is only a little boy and there is lots of things to clean it. One day he will grow up and be on his own and it won't matter. This a true story for sure. Stefan was not to blame, he was a little boy who was encouraged by, and thought he was pleasing, his grandfather. Today, Stefan is 38 and that incident does not matter at all. It only adds to memories. When he was 20 and attending Saint Mary's University, we were having dinner one day. "Dad, I still miss my Pop Mitchell sometimes."

How did Tom make such a wonderful impression on him as a little boy that he still loves his grandfather after all these years? Even today, he remembers and cherishes his memories. But the memories are fading. He says that sometimes he is not sure if he actually remembers some things or some are stories told by others as he grew up. I hope all children are so lucky with their grandfathers.

I remember when Stefan was old enough to start school. The night before his first day, he was sent upstairs to bed at about 8:30 P.M. and tucked in with prayers and kisses good night as usual. At about 11 P.M. Sharon and I were watching TV downstairs and I said to Sharon, "I think I hear Stefan moving around upstairs." I went up to his room and he was standing in the window, looking toward the school where he was to go in the morning.

"Stefan, what is the problem?" I asked.

With tears in his eyes he stated, "I am just a little boy, dad, but I have to go to school tomorrow."

It was a special moment indeed. It broke my heart really. With that I scooped him up in my arms, cuddled him close and said, "I think you will be fine. You are not a little boy anymore, you are a big boy now. Besides, Mom and I will take you there and ensure you are safe, and we will pick you up to take you home every day. Pretty soon you will have many new friends and will want to go to school on your own."

I tucked him back into bed with a hug, kiss and a good a night story. At about 3 A.M., he woke up and found his way to our bed. He climbed in and cuddled down behind my back. I turned over toward him and placed my arm around him. Off to sleep we went, all was well and safe now.

I tried to spend time with my kids as they were growing up. Was I a perfect father? Probably not, but I always did the best I could. As in life in general, it is good to always do the best one can. Today, Stefan has a good life in Halifax and works in construction. After wasting a few years and some money at Saint Mary's University he has found his niche in life working with his hands and really enjoys what he does. It was probably a seed set by his grandfather Tom.

# CHAPTER FIFTEEN

As I earlier stated, my daughter Suzanne was born July 30, 1982. Some of my best memories of Suzanne are picking her and Mary Healy up after sea cadets each week and dropping Mary at home. I would then take Suzanne to Tim Horton's for hot chocolate, a ginger bread person and a father daughter chat. The gingerbread cookies were named gingerbread men at that time, but she refused to call them "men," only gingerbread persons. She would say to the server, "I want a gingerbread person please. Can you put pink icing on it?" They would add pink icing buttons. "Good for her," I said.

One of my favourite stories about Suzanne is her butterfly sandwiches. In Newfoundland at the time, there was a product called Fusel's Cream — it was a thick, rich cream. The product can had a gold butterfly on the label. Suzanne liked to have this cream spread on a piece of bread. Her Uncle Shawn would say there was a butterfly in the can. I am making you a butterfly sandwich, he would say. Whenever her Uncle Shawn would ask her if she would like a butterfly sandwich, her usual answer was "Yes, Uncle Shawn." Soon Suzanne was also asking for a butterfly sandwich. Uncle Shawn would get her to watch him opening the can to watch for the butterfly. Every time he made her a Fussell's Cream sandwich she would just stare intently as the can was opened to see that butterfly that must be inside to pop out. No matter how hard she tried, she never did see that butterfly, of course. There were not any butterflies in the can, it was just her Uncle Shawn playing a game with her. Both of them enjoyed it. I think Shawn more than her.

Today, Suzanne is 35 and, on occasion, she still laughingly and lovingly talks about that butterfly sandwich and how intently she watched. Don't you just love kids and their imagination? It is truly amazing, and they love to believe in possibilities. What happens to us as we become adults? Why do we lose our imagination and belief in possibilities?

Suzanne enjoyed piano and progressed up to grade eight at The Royal Conservatory of Music when we lived in Saint John, New Brunswick, and Halifax. Piano training also took place in Marystown during our years living there. Two piano teachers she really liked were Mr. Neil Power, a local musician, and her mother's Aunt Ita. Those two are loved by all the people who know them. Both had played in bands during their lives and also were invited to many local Newfoundland house parties where they often played impromptu jam sessions for hours at a time.

I usually took Suzanne figure skating Saturday mornings because her mother worked at a local bank that required working on Saturday mornings, usually until early afternoon. One memory that gives me warm feelings is at her figure skating class, especially at the end. The bird dance song and music was always played for all the kids to dance. Suzanne really loved that, she always looked forward to it. As soon as it started to play her face would light up, she immediately looked toward me to ensure I was there and watching, which I always was. She was so happy then — great smiles and laughs. It really made her dad's heart melt and smile all at once. Other moms and dads dropped the kids off to figure skating and disappeared, showing up when class was over. Oh, what they missed. Future Canadian Champion and Olympic medalist, Katlin Osborn, would later attend this figure skating club. She probably also did the bird dance at a young age.

As my stroke recovery went forward, I received little quotes of positive thinking from Suzanne. These were just to let me know she was thinking of me and loved her dad. My plan was to add those quotes here but I could not find who the authors were. Even Googling the quotes did not reveal the authors. I liked them, and I know I have loved her even before she was born and have ever since. Just a few days ago I found a CD she gave me when she was a teenager. There's only one song on it: Butterfly kisses. As I played it for the first time in years I remembered her childhood and her growing up. Choking back my tears, I uttered the words: "I love you so much Suzanne, my little girl." I have copied this song to the IPod that I have in my SUV and will hear it a lot more in the days, weeks, months and years ahead.

Just recently I was having lot of pain and issues with my back. It was painful just to bend to tie my shoes. Suzanne noticed my pain and rushed over, kneeling on the floor in front of me. She said, "Dad I can tie those. You tied my shoes many times when I was a little girl."

"I sure did," I replied.

Aww, a special moment.

I am not sure why but it was a little embarrassing not being able to tie my own shoes and it was an emotional moment for me. Later, when I thought about it, tears filled my eyes. It really was a special moment.

"There you are dad," she said with a smile as she finished tying my shoes. "Let me know if you need your shoes tied again. Rest your back or even walk a while, that will help make it better."

"Thank you honey, I love you," I said.

"I love you too, Dad," she replied.

My thought was I must have done something right. It is the little things that mean so much sometimes.

# CHAPTER SIXTEEN

Soon after Suzanne was born, Tom was diagnosed with cancer. In 1982, as he got sicker, Tom asked to come to stay with us. Sharon was the eldest daughter and his favourite (I think). She was the only one who would consider having him around all the time considering his history. With two small children, this was a tall order for us. He ended up moving in with us and I am not sure who benefited the most: Tom, or Stefan and Suzanne. Tom so loved spending time with them. Many times when Tom was feeling ill, he would stay in bed and Stefan would go into his papa's room and get into bed with him. Tom loved this of course. They chatted and told stories. Stefan was happy when this happened and it was good for Tom also. I also had many chats with Tom over the period of his illness. He seemed to be at peace with it all and knew he was facing death, although he did not plan to give up easy. Tom told us many times he was happy he could stay with us.

Suzanne also got to know her grandfather at a very young age, but unfortunately she does not remember it today. We have told her about him as she grew up. e

Just before Christmas 1982, Tom grew very ill. The cancer had spread to his brain and he was hospitalized. It did not look good. After few days, he grew progressively worse and slipped into a coma on the Saturday evening just before Christmas. Tom's brother and two sisters came to stay with him at the hospital all night at his bedside. On Sunday morning, I went to the hospital to sit with Tom. I was sitting alone with him at his bedside at 11 A.M. when he drew his last breath. Suddenly, he sat up in his bed, looked around, and asked me what I was doing there. He then fell back on the bed. His breathing became much laboured, he was gasping for breath. It was hard to watch, but his man would not die alone, I was there with him. I remember there was a hymn called "Safe in the Arms of Jesus" playing on the local radio station. Please learn to forgive. It will lighten the load you are carrying through this life.

I have found the courage to forgive my mother for her abuse. Staying angry at a person is like letting them control your thoughts and allowing them to live in your head rent free for years. When you forgive, a weight is lifted from you, you are free. There's no point to carry it for one's whole life. It is a no win for anyone, certainly not me. It's best to forgive and move on. It is OK to forgive even if one will never forget. It is Ok! One does not have to forget. Forgiveness is freeing indeed, it is golden. I came to realize my mother probably did the best she could. She could not give what she did not have because nobody gave it to her. Mother, you were not a great mother, but I forgive you for your short comings.

After Tom passed I went to advise his family and then on to his house to check on things such as suit. Tom's oldest son, Vincent, and oldest daughter, Sharon, made funeral arrangements. On arriving at Tom's house I noted the house was deathly quiet, the clock on the wall had stopped the exact minute Tom had died but was still plugged into the electric outlet. I tapped the clock and it restarted. I also noted that the house was very cold although the thermostats showed the electric heat was turned on. I checked the wall heaters but these were cold. I checked the power panel — it was ok, and I tapped the thermostats, which immediately engaged the heaters to give off their heat to warm the freezing-cold house. The whole experience made me feel uneasy, really.

While living in this house in later years, we would hear somebody walking on the upstairs floor at night after the kids were asleep. At first when we started to hear those noises we would go upstairs to check on our kids. They were always asleep in their beds, but we always had a feeling somebody was there but not visible. Sometimes we would catch a glimpse of a man moving about, but eventually we stopped going upstairs to check. Sharon would say "Dad is checking on Stefan and Suzanne again." He sure was. Now in my own life I am calm about the thought of death. Because of my own experiences, I do not fear death anymore. A quote from myself: "Dying is not the end, it is just the beginning."

**A quote from Grace Hanson:**

*"Don't be afraid your life will end; be afraid it will never end."*

# CHAPTER SEVENTEEN

After being laid-off from the Marystown Shipyard. It was a dead end job, and I lived in a place where I would have to struggle through my whole life financially, probably receiving EI most of the rest of my life. I did not want that. I made a tough decision, the only possible positive decision for my family's life going forward. I decided to return to school. I researched a program that I thought would be most beneficial and could also possibly use some of the skills I had already acquired. I was able to find such a program at the College of the North Atlantic (CONA), an extension of Memorial University. I was ready for training for a more technical career. I applied for a program entitled Welding Engineering Tech through a Canada Manpower grant (now named Services Canada Training Grant). There were discussions as to my math skills at the time. I didn't learn algebra or calculus when I was in high school, so I was given a date and time to attend a math skill test at CONA. I really needed to do well to be able to attend the college program I wanted. This test did not go well. I needed 50% minimum but I fell just a couple of points short. After getting a lower than the required score, the advice I received was my math skills were not up to par to continue to study the program. I made an appointment to talk to my case worker at Canada Manpower and also another appointment to talk to the college president. I was adamant to them that I could do this if they let me give it a shot at least one semester. I promised them at the end of that semester that if my grades are lacking, I will leave the program on my own, and pay back any money spent by the Canadian Government Service Centre. If I do fine and my grades are good, then I can continue.

"Nobody has ever said that to me," the man said. "I think you will do just fine, I believe in you and am willing to give you the chance you need to make your life better."

"I will not let you or my family down on this one," I said.

I started the program in September that year, studied and worked hard for two years and graduated with a 3.87 grade point out of a possible 4.0. Not bad indeed. I eventually passed my Level 3 CWB Inspector certification and then some NDE CGSB certifications. I have worked in the quality control or Quality Assurance field since then, and sometimes in the engineering departments, as a Field Engineer on projects advising engineers on QA and FRP issues. I have worked on many large construction projects such as oil and nickel refineries, oil and gas infrastructure projects, building offshore oil and gas drilling and extraction platforms, many types of ships, bridges, barges, Alberta Canada oil sands development projects etc. I have really enjoyed working in that field of expertise. If you love what you do it is said then you will never work a day in your life. I have enjoyed so much that I feel I have not really worked a day since my career started on that path, although I did get paid well. I started a small business in 2007 contracting myself out as a consultant to large, multi- billion dollar projects in the mining and oil and gas industry.

My career, my company, my income and my health all came crashing down when my serious health condition knocked me down in March 2015. My stroke and subsequent brain surgery, resulted in a disability of having to live with a brain injury. For two years I felt scared, frustrated, hurt, angry, betrayed and sometimes even desperate about what had happened to me, but those times are getting fewer as time moves forward. Today I have a problem performing Grade 5 math. That is difficult mentally to accept, but it is what I have to do. I go forward each day, no matter what. I am lucky my memory is great, I still remember codes, how to read drawings and all of my previous work life and experiences. However, my days of climbing around in large or small tanks are over, but then again, I am 61 years old now.

# CHAPTER EIGHTEEN

In July or August of 2015 I learned I had been married a second time. Although my memory is really great, for some reason I could not remember much about her. Sometimes people are best forgotten about, but unfortunately, my memory of her did return as time went on.

I got married in late 2006, separated late 2010, and divorced in early 2011. Sandy always wore a mask. I look back now and I realize I never really knew her, maybe nobody did because she very rarely, if ever, revealed her true self. She always kept her real self behind a façade, a mask

To me, she seemed to be a genuine good and fairly happy woman. We seemed to get along very well (at least at first). After we were married she changed, as is often the case after the dating turns to marriage and living together.

Her focus seemed to be mostly on herself and money. At the time we married I was making great money as the Nova Scotia Division Regional Manager of a good company. I planned dinners out, vacations and any weekends away, and was expected to pay for it all. This was a stress on me.

Sandy's parents had moved back to Italy prior to us meeting. They live in a village near Teramo, in the Abruzzo region. Sandy and I travelled to Italy on a few occasions. Her parents always treated me well; they are good, kind people. We stayed in Italy as long as vacations allowed, and we did some travel around the country (at my expense, of course). Sometimes I was stressed about the financial cost of it all, but she was not paying so she never gave it a thought. We visited such places as Florence and other areas in the Tuscany Region, Venice, Cinque Terra, Naples, Sorrento, the Amalfi Coast, Capri, Pompeii, Solarno, Rome, Pescara, Saint Gabriele, Casino, Pisa, Teramo, L'Aquila, L'Spezia, many mountain villages and coastal beach towns, many old churches (like the Vatican in Rome, Saint Marks in Venice, etc.). We did a lot of sightseeing to get the flavour of Italy. We enjoyed the travelling.

During the time I was with her, my daughter, Suzanne, joined the military. One day after I had not seen her for close to two years, she called stating that she and her boyfriend were coming home for Christmas and would be staying with us. I was elated and told Sandy the good news, but she was not happy for me. She portrayed a "Who cares?" attitude, even saying she did not want my daughter to stay with us. That made me very upset. Did she really think I was going to tell my daughter not to come home for Christmas? I told

Sandy that Suzanne would be coming home and I couldn't wait to see her.

During Suzanne's visit Sandra made me feel guilty about having her around. She was jealous or envious it seems. I think the visit went well, but then I was not concerned about what Sandy thought. I shrugged it off, but I was not going to miss a Christmas with my daughter whom was away serving her country as a soldier, and whom I had not seen for some time. I just wanted us to have Christmas together as a family.

Sandra's behavior did put a strain on our relationship and it made me really question her intentions. Who was this woman? Today I believe I did not ever really know her, nor did anybody for that matter. She always wore a mask. Now I look back and realize I thought about this Christmas incident many times and it really bothered me. It was difficult to think my wife wanted to keep my daughter and me apart at Christmas for her own selfish reasons. Having said that she did seem to enjoy the season anyway. I am glad I did not cave to Sandy's demands. During the time I was with Sandy, my kids and I became further apart. She did not like them around, but I still tried to keep things together with them. I am happy we later divorced. At least I have a great relationship with my son and daughter now.

One day about three years into our marriage I noticed the engagement ring I gave her when I proposed did not look exactly right — it did not look to be the same ring. I asked her about it and apparently she had removed the diamond and had replaced it with a much larger, fake diamond, a

Cubic Zirconia. I was very hurt by that and disappointed in her. I felt betrayed. Sandy had never discussed it with me — never even mentioned it to me — and I found out by accident. For once she revealed her true self, her true identity: materialistic, deceitful and dishonest. I wondered what other things were kept hidden behind her facade. I had given her the ring to show my love for her and our love for each other. It was a ring I had designed and had gotten a local Halifax jeweller to make for her. I had emptied out my savings account to pay cash for it, and I had put a lot thought into my proposal to her. She was very happy with it the day I proposed. Then in later months I remembered her talking about some of her clients sporting and bragging about the size of their diamond. Women can be very shallow about a diamond engagement ring. The size of an engagement ring does not translate into the size of love between couples, or bragging rights. She obviously was very envious of others' rings and was a shallow, materialistic person.

"Sandy, that is the ring I proposed to you with," I said. "Nothing should be able to replace that ring." I know some folks that did not have an engagement ring but loved each other for a lifetime, until death parted them.

"Sure it may not be as large as some of your clients'," I said, "but it is our ring that symbolizes our love — not others — but down the road at a special anniversary celebration of a number of years married I may have been able to upgrade it to a much bigger diamond. The ring you are now wearing has absolutely no meaning for me, for us. It is just a fake, and maybe you and our marriage is a fake also."

I was so disappointed and hurt that I never got that act of dishonesty and deceit out of my mind. I could not believe that anyone would actually do that — I had never heard of that before in my life, nor have I heard of it since. It's so disappointing and I think that was the beginning of the end for me and us. Who does that? She and I became more distant as time went on. I tried to reach her, reach us, but it seemed to be impossible. As most do, after a while, I also began to give up on her. We were giving up on each other and I then began to think that maybe I would be best without her.

Personally, I do not have photos of her. A woman who was a close friend of ours told me I was too nice a guy for my ex-wife.

My children tell me they did not like Sandy much. She was not a nice person, was jealous of them and was not good for me, while I was a friendly type who got along with others very well, even people I did not know. They tell me she was a selfish, distant woman. Although I did not listen to them at the time, they were right.

Thank God I was finally coming to my senses.

Soon, my second guessing became stronger. Maybe this woman is not for me. Maybe I would be better off alone or to find a more suitable woman to share life with. This thinking really bothered me because at one point I had loved this woman. I had not thought about divorce until now, so I prayed about it, but it seemed not to help very much. Today

I conclude maybe God had a different plan for me, a better plan. I am sure he did. I think I could have gotten through it but one day after an argument, we decided maybe we should separate. I asked if we needed counselling of some sort or if she thought that would be a good idea, but she refused all help. I was a little taken back and I stated that we may as well go the full way and file for divorce. There's no need to go through life not happy. She then came up with a plan that she could live with: divorce, live separately but stay together as a couple. One night I sat on the couch next to her, placed my arm around her and leaned over to kiss her. During the kiss, I suddenly removed my arms from around her, broke the kiss, got up from the couch and said, "I think it is time for me to go. I think this is over." And that was that, I walked out the door. It was done, I was done. Oh, it was hard emotionally for a while, as break ups are, but sometimes one just has to find the strength to do what is best. I was the opposite of her and opposites do attract sometimes as they say.

Many people are in bad marriages and bad relationships because they lack the strength to do the right and necessary thing — save themselves.

Half divorced does not work well. Save yourself the grief. A clean break can restart life; a new beginning is best. Proverbs 16:9: "A man's heart deviseth his way but the Lord directeth his steps."

There is one thing I know for sure: one cannot change the past, cannot rewind it or re-live it. They can change how their past affects them by changing their thoughts and their thinking. No use dwelling on the past; let it go as you have to let each day go to allow yourself to fall to sleep each night. Let the day go, let your hurtful past go, forgive, lay it at the foot of the cross, ask Jesus to carry it for you, then let it go, knowing you do not have to carry it anymore, you have passed it to Jesus. I have done this many times when going through my many life's difficult challenges.

# CHAPTER NINETEEN

My life has not been an easy road, it has often been very difficult. Since the day I was born, I have been trying to thread the needle of life and on a few occasions I have had success. My life has also been sprinkled with the occasional good fortune and some great days that never seemed to last long enough. Mostly it has been difficult. During my working life, I tried to plan well to have a financially stress-free retirement around 63 years old. I was once told, if you want to make God laugh tell him your plans. He has his own plan for me and for you.

I was almost 59 by the time I realized that maybe my life was never meant to be easy. At times I have felt angry about my circumstance, but have let it go and accepted life as it is. I have accepted that this is the way life is for me, so it seems. Just at or near retirement, life takes a nasty down turn, as it has for other folks I have worked with. I do know some of those folks well and I am sure my readers know people also whose lives were given an unexpected curve ball just as they approached retirement. My life took a dramatic change for the worse, a life curve ball in March 2015 just four and a half years prior to my planned retirement dates when I was hit with a stroke and brain surgery.

# CHAPTER TWENTY

My type of contract work led me to the pinnacle of my career to signature a contract agreement to work as a consultant for a large Brazilian mining company called Vale. Vale was in the process of building a nickel refinery in the middle of nowhere — the town of Long Harbour, Newfoundland. This place may not be the end of the world but you can see the end of the earth from here. Long Harbour is a small Newfoundland out port town. Even I had never been to this town before, although it is only a three-hour drive from where I grew up. Long Harbour, I would soon learn, has a lot of rain, drizzle and fog, better known as RDF. I think this place produced RDF and shipped to the rest of Canada's east coast. Common weather were strong winds, horizontal rain, lots of fog. In winter it was common to see horizontal snow and many winter storms — it was a miserable weather place. On one occasion it rained for so many days in a row, it was depressing. The rain started the day I arrived back from my seven-day-off rotation. I worked 14/7: fourteen days on site and seven days off. It was raining the day I arrived and was still raining the day I left. After another two weeks of RDF and much complaining from me and most people on the project site, I came up with an idea for a song, so I wrote it. Here are a few verses to give you a flavour:

**The Long Harbour Depression**

I wake up in the morning
Getting ready for the day
Rain falling on my window
Looking out across the bay

Every day it seems to rain
Workplace problems too many to name
Like a movie, sad to say
Every day is Groundhog Day

It's raining in Long Harbour today
Yes it's raining in Long Harbour again
Where the sun hardly shines
There's bad weather most of the time
Yes, it's raining in Long Harbour again.

The Vale project site and the town of Long Harbour are located close to the shores of the Atlantic Ocean. Long Harbour is a deep, well protected, beautiful harbour at the end of the beautiful, large ocean bay called Placentia Bay. This is where the ocean becomes a shoreline. On arriving to work for Vale, the person responsible for housing gave me the keys to a small but nice two-bedroom mini home to live in temporarily, as part of my contract. This mini home was half way up a steep hill on a side road. I would really enjoy working at this project for more than three years until my health issues changed all that in March 2015.

I arrived at Long Harbour on November 30, 2012. Shortly after dinner one chilly, early-December evening a few days after arrival, I decided to go for a walk just to see this very small out port town, to get some air, and to get my mind of the stresses of my new job. As I was walking along I noticed an older gentleman stringing up Christmas lights on and about his house. As I walked past the house, he came walking toward me. Now, I did not know this person, nor had I ever seen him before, but having been born in Newfoundland, I had an idea of what was coming next.

"How you doing, Skipper?" he said. Skipper is a Newfoundland word used to greet a friend. "You working up there?" he said, pointing in the direction of the Vale project site.

"Yes I am," I said.

"Come on in for a drink, my son," he said.

"Well, I do not drink much," I said.

"Well you are in luck," he said, "because I do not have a lot to drink. I only have two 40s of rum — enough to last for an hour or so."

I smiled and answered "Yes, I will have a drink."

And we went inside. He soon poured a drink of rum for himself, then handed the bottle to me.

"Pour your own my son," he said. "Help yourself, we do not tend on anybody, you got to help yourself around here. Even the misses don't tend on me either so help yourself to a drink. If you're hungry there's lots of food in the fridge. Help yourself my son."

"Tend on" is a Newfoundland word that means serving somebody. We had a good conversation, or as Newfoundlanders say, "a good yarn," but it could have lasted for hours. The guy was constantly pointing to the bottle of rum and my glass, "Come on bye, drink her up. There is another one where that came from."

He wanted me to refill my glass, and occasionally he would pick up the bottle of rum and motion to fill my glass himself. I placed my open hand over the top my glass to stop him, but the word no was not understood it seemed. He soon just poured the rum onto the back of my hand.

"Let that good stuff seep down into the glass, bye. It will warm you up," he said.

Newfoundlanders are very friendly and accommodating people that work hard, are smart, are very wise and have a lot of passion for life. They love a good chat; it is just their normal way of life in a small out port town in Newfoundland. The television is switched off when a person enters your house, there's a good chat and storytelling, and maybe even a song or two becomes the evening entertainment.

I had been living in Mainland Canada for some time now but still understood his thick Newfoundland accent and his slang. He said things such as: "It is a little duckish out, my son", or "Where do you belong to?" That meant he was asking me where was I was born and grew up and duckish means it is dusk or getting dark outside. I told him I was originally from Creston South, or Marystown as it is named due to town amalgamation.

"Down on the south coast on the Burin Peninsula," I said. "I grew up and lived there before moving to the mainland some time ago."

He slapped me on the back and said, well! "Welcome back home, my son. Why would anybody want to leave Newfoundland?" he said. "I don't understand it, but they all go eventually. It seems especially the young ones going looking for work, I suppose. Lots of work around here now even the mainlanders are flying to Newfoundland. The young ones go to Alberta and all over the place, more stuff to do there I suppose. Eventually they all will find their way home again, if not to stay then probably every year for vacation time. They just can't stay away because once Newfoundland is in your blood, it is your roots, and it calls you back again and again."

"That is true," I said "and many start a family where they decide to work and settle a while. They stay away but eventually return as they get older. Some come back home to retire."

I was soon excusing myself and on my way, but this gentleman wanted me to stay.

"No rush," he said often, offering me another drink as I was leaving. As I continued on my way with a smile from ear to ear, my thoughts were about how this fellow did not know who I was and did not care. He was just being his friendly, inviting, own self. That would never happen in any other place in Canada, I thought, only in small town Newfoundland. It gave me a wonderful feeling of being home. I had not felt that in a long time. Every time that gentleman saw me after that he greeted me like I was his best buddy.

As I walked along the only community road I noticed a community hall. Although I did not know at the time, this would be a place I would visit over the next few years for evenings of Irish Newfoundland music, "Screeching In's" for folks from away to become an honorary Newfoundlander, comedy evenings of skits and such. Evening get-togethers, including dances like the Newfoundland waltz and the tap dance. I had learned these dances as a boy while my father played his button accordion that laid across his knee. And Grandmother Crocker played her Piano accordion in our house. Vale arranged other evenings for special celebrations, which included meals prepared by the local town folks. Many locals were welcome and attended those evening gatherings. All were welcome. As a Newfoundlander would describe it; "A great time, my son." These evenings will always hold a special place in my heart and for many folks I knew at the project site. I still get emails from as far away as Vancouver Canada, North and South Carolina, Texas USA, England and Africa reminiscing about those evenings. They are truly wonderful and great memories.

The "Screeching In" ceremony is common in Newfoundland for non-Newfoundlanders. During this ceremony, usually one is dressed in a yellow rain gear jacket and pants — or "oil skins" as Newfoundlanders refer to them — a pair of rubbers at least up to their knees and a sou'wester. They're given a Newfoundland name, such as Paddy Bye or Garge. They get a shot glass of screech straight up, eat a piece of bologna, kiss the cod fish, get tapped on the shoulder with an oar from a dory, and are baptised as an honorary Newfoundlander along with a few jokes thrown in. The ceremonies also include lots of comedy. After the ceremony, each participant is given an honorary Newfoundlander certificate with their new honorary Newfoundland name. Although this is a fun evening which everyone enjoys, it is taken seriously by Newfoundlanders. Newfoundlanders holding a ceremony usually have to apply to the government liquor commission for Screeching In certificates prior to the ceremony. For the ceremony to be valid, only native Newfoundlanders are allowed to perform it.

My mini home was very windy at night when the wind blew, which was most nights. The place just rattled. It was not a place for nervous folks for sure, but I was ok there. Sometimes I thought I was going to be blown away and find myself somewhere out the harbour in the morning.

There were not many people around the place that I knew, so I was lonely sometimes, especially in the evening after work. Later in the summer of 2012 I was given accommodations at the Vale-owned Long Harbour Lodge. I lived at the lodge in Long Harbour during my 14-day work rotation until my health issues began in March 2015. I resided along with approximately 40 other men. A few women also resided at the lodge on occasion, but they seemed to move on sooner than most. We treated women the same as the rest, no different. She had a job to do and was welcomed to sit at the guys table also. Usually, these women sat at the dinner table with guys and women they were working with on the project site or knew prior to arriving. Meals were provided by the worst cook in Newfoundland, the head chef. On some weekday evenings from the windows of the second-floor room or dining area windows, or if one happened to wander into the dining area at the time, a car could be seen parked at the back door of the kitchen area. A person could be seen loading grocery items into his car before leaving for the day. The cook used a lot of salt to put a taste on his food or mask the taste, depending on who you ask. The cook was a really good guy, very friendly and welcoming as are most Newfoundlanders. The cooking he did for me was easy. Usually I only ate two fried egg whites and a bowl of porridge with raisins for breakfast. If there was a plan to cook red meat or ham for dinner, I requested the cook have some fish, salmon or haddock ready for me. This he obligingly did on many days for me with a smile, no problem. He was not a great cook but a good guy indeed. Usually there was a different cook on weekends. This guy could cook. He was a great guy also. He always said, "I am rebel like you, George." One of the women usually cooked Sunday dinner, which was always a good meal. The weekend cooks told us not to praise up the weekend meals too much because the Head Chef would get jealous and not let them cook anymore. The lodge had a few local women working in the kitchen as servers and kitchen help. All the lodge staff were local folks. Any local person that wanted a job had a job during this project. Most were working at the project site in the trades or another area they were qualified for.

There was a local small convenience store that we referred to as "Going to the mall" and it was the shopping outing. Now this store was not very convenient for folks that normally lived in a city, but it did sell beer. That's just what one needs in a boring little town: folks getting drunk for something to do, and starting the next work day with a hangover. As for me, I have never drank much alcohol in my life. There were a few guys that I became friends with, Terry from Grand Falls, NL but living in Halifax, NS, and Carl from St. Lawrence, NL where he was born and still lives. There was Ricky from the Philippines but living in Toronto, Ontario, Nick from Italy but living in Thomson, Manitoba. All of us are still friends today even after the project finished. We stay in contact regularly. Nick and I became good buddies. Nick was a little cheap when buying things. He loved a glass of wine but only would buy the cheapest. We did have a little fun staying at the lodge among all the residents. There was nothing else to do so I would tease him with a wine that had good flavour, a top-shelf wine that was a little more expensive than the stuff would purchase. Nick usually only got the bottom shelf cheap stuff, I jokingly teased him. Wine was sold at many local area gas stations along with any other alcohol available in Newfoundland. These gas stations also had walk-in coolers for cold beer. After some months, Nick called my room saying he had a top-shelf wine and asked me to come up for a glass.

On occasion a few of us would gather in a friends room, usually Terry Kelly's, for a glass of whatever you enjoyed to drink. Those that could, played guitar (usually just me). Some evenings we would listen and watch Johnny Cash concert videos. Those get-togethers usually happened Friday or Saturday evening, until 11 P.M. when all headed back to our own room for the night, feeling great, tired and sleepy.

My routine was to get up at 6 A.M. for breakfast, then to the project site to start work at 7 A.M. through to 5:30 P.M. daily. It was 10 hours of work plus a half hour or so for lunch. This was the routine for the entire 14-day rotation shift. Ten hours paid work a day at the project site, 70 hours a week, 140 hours for the 14 days. Sometimes when necessary a few more hours got added as required to meet a schedule.

Those were mostly good times on those evenings at the lodge, but it could also get lonely on occasion. The Vale employees staying at the lodge came to know Anne Whiffen and her husband, Aldo, who both worked on the project. Anne and Aldo were very good folks and friendly. They were typical Newfoundlanders and would occasionally have a gathering at their house for some project personnel, inviting their friends. I always went and brought my guitar, and occasionally Dan Donnelly showed up and also played guitar a little. Those get-togethers were good for the lodge residents, and some Vale folks from project who came. On occasion other work friends of Anne and Aldo also were invited and came. We usually looked forward to those little parties. No TV was visible, just conversation, laughs, good food, a few drinks, music and friends. The evening usually turned into a sing along if the folks knew the song being played. "Music, food, a few drinks and friends go together," as Newfoundlanders say.

Anne and Aldo were so wonderful — real friends. I still talk to Anne on occasion, checking via email and the occasional phone call, just to stay in touch and inquire about how things are with her and Aldo. She still works with Vale at the nickel refinery after its completion, as they're now in production phase. I am told Aldo has retired and Anne will retire soon. Their daughter has given birth to a son, their first grandchild. They are so happy and proud about that, and sometimes we exchange photos of our grandchildren. I am sure on any future visits to Newfoundland I will drop by for a visit. Anne and Aldo could warm even the iciest hearts. True Newfoundlanders indeed. Long Harbour has the friendliest people that can be found anywhere. That helped offset the bad weather.

During the weeks at the lodge, I went to the gym every second night, paddled a stationary bike for an hour, and also lifted a few weights. Maybe three or four other people went to the gym as well. When a new person came to stay at the lodge, they usually came also but after a few days their gym visits got fewer. Most evenings there was just me and one other guy, Larry, from Cape Breton, Nova Scotia.

For meals, it was usually the same people that sat together all the time, breakfast, lunch and dinner. Usually it was folks that were working together, so they'd discuss the day's work, work problems, tell stories and just joke around. That was good for morale and friendship also. We got to know each other and families through conversation. There was one great rule: no mobile phones were allowed at meals, none at the table.

Nick, my Italian friend, can be very passionate when talking about work, especially his speciality: the Fiberglass Reinforced Plastics (FRP). We drove together for the 15-minute drive from the lodge to the project site and the return ride. We also worked together often on the project site. I knew some of the Italian language because of my marriage to Sandy. I had taken some Italian lessons and I would joke with Nick because — like most Italians — when he spoke his hands always were moving with great expression.

"Nick, the only way to keep an Italian quiet is to tie his hands in his pockets," I would jokingly say.

"That's right buddy," he would say, laughing.

As soon as he was in my car for the drive back from the project site his voice was usually raised, talking passionately about the day's issues, complaining about people he had issues with. Of course I would argue with him when I thought he was wrong, and so it went. Upon hearing his complaints day after day this behavior played on my nerves a bit. One evening we were driving from work toward the lodge for the night, and suddenly I stopped the car and yelled at Nick to

"Get the hell out, buddy." He was surprised to hear that. He looked over at me and said, "You do not mean that buddy, do you?" I started to laugh and drove on. Upon leaving the work site I stopped at the security gate, rolled down his window, and told him to hang all his grievances on the gate post. We will stop in the morning coming back for you to pick them up again, I told him. Nick and I have had many laughs about that incident. After that whenever he got in my car to return from the work site he sat down then motioned his fingers to his lips saying zip it, OK then. I told him it is good to discuss work issues but do it in a calm way. After that dust up all went well and we became closer buddies.

Nick, me and sometimes a few other guys who stayed at the lodge liked to go to the nearby town of Placentia. It is a really beautiful little Newfoundland out port town in Placentia Bay. There is a bar located there by the name of "The Three Sisters" that served food every day. It was a good place to go for dinner sometimes just for a change. There was a Karaoke bar on Friday nights. Nick and I nicknamed this bar "The Six Tits" — three sisters, six tits, get it? This name began to stick with the project folks who also frequented the bar. It was a good place to go to have a drink, listen to music and unwind a little. There were a few locals and project folks, singers that performed every week — some good, others not so good, as is true with most Karaoke. The idea is to have fun and we did. Two locals, Andy and his wife, stood out from the rest. Andy was a fan of George Jones, and sang most of those George Jones songs. He had a good voice if one likes country music and Andy even cried when he talked about the death of George Jones. On many Friday nights, Nick and I went to the Karaoke bar and I would always buy Andy and his wife a beer or whatever drink they preferred. Andy always wore a black George Jones tee shirt. On one occasion I noted Andy was not there so I asked the young lady bartender where he was. "He's home washing his t-shirt," she said with a big, beautiful smile. Newfoundlanders do have a since of humour.

On the second week I was in hospital, Nick skipped work one Saturday, got up about 4 A.M., and drove to St. John's about 2 hours away. He then boarded a two-hour flight to Halifax, Nova Scotia to visit me for the day. He then took a return flight late that evening back to Newfoundland. Although I still had a lot of recovery to do, Nancy got me out of hospital on a weekend pass for his visit. It was good therapy for me and I felt better than I had in weeks.

We had a great day together and he's a real friend indeed. Not many would do that, in fact no others did. Nick is retired now and has to return to the South of Italy l this year. We talk often and he is currently looking to buy a villa there in his hometown where he has two sons. One son is a policeman, the other son is a lawyer. Nick now has two grandchildren. He would rather live alone than with his kids he said, I understand that. Nick was divorced many years ago and did not remarry. His ex-wife went home to Scotland. Nick and his sons have not seen or heard from her since. I plan to go visit him for a month or two next year in Italy. It will be great — old friends together again.

**Early morning mist on Long Harbour early fall morning**

**Town of Long Harbour**

**View of a threatening sky driving into Long Harbour**

# CHAPTER TWENTY-ONE

*E*arly after my admission to hospital, during the time I was asleep from anesthetic after coming out of surgery, I had an experience that would take greater meaning to me as time went on. I remember being visited by people from the spirit world. First, there were two young men who visited me. They were sitting on chairs next to my bed talking to me.

"I know you guys, but you guys are dead. What are you doing here?"

One was Clifford Bennet, a friend who had died while we were in high school. The other was my brother, Fraser, who was killed in a car accident at age 25 in 1972 in Burin Bay, where he lived. I was 16 at the time, but this person was a younger version of him, about the same age as he was when he fell over a Cliff in Burin Bay at age 16. He was in Whale Cove, located in Burin Bay, cutting wood with our brother-in-law who lived there. The ground near a steep cliff gave away causing him to fall down the cliff. He grabbed for the sides as he fell, tearing away the tops of his fingers on the jagged rocks. The fall also gave him many bumps and bruises, a few small broken bones, and a head injury. He was patched up at the local hospital and then rushed to St John's Hospital for treatment. At this hospital, he spent some months recovering before returning home, Fraser did not speak to me. WHY?! I later wondered. I think it was because, the decision would have been harder. Cliff pointed his finger at me and said, "We know we are dead but we were sent to get you, take you with us."

"Tell me where," I said, but they did not answer. "I do not want to go," I said.

They soon left my side.

Soon after they had gone, my Uncle Lenard and his wife, Ester, visited me from the spirit world. Uncle Lenard and Auntie Ester would stay at my house in Newfoundland during visits from Australia. Uncle Lenard lived in Australia most of his life and his life would make a book in itself. His wife was from New Zealand. Uncle Leonard joined the Merchant Marines in Halifax, Nova Scotia, back in the early 1940s. Later in World War II, his ship was torpedoed while bringing supplies to the troops. While staying at my home, he told me he was rescued and brought to a hospital in New Zealand where Ester was a nurse. They met, eventually married and later moved to Australia.

"What are you guys doing here?" I asked my uncle.

"We came to get you," he said.

He told me all was going to be OK, but I told him that I was staying. They seemed very peaceful and happy. I was really talking to these people — they were standing next to me. It was so real, God was talking to me. I woke up when I said, "No I am not going." What did this mean? I have concluded I was in dire straits and was given a choice. If I had agreed to go would I have died? Possibly, but who knows for sure. I did not find out.

On a more humorous side, I told this story to my oldest nephew, James, who laughed and stated "If you were going with Uncle Lenard you must have been going the wrong way." I believe I had been given a choice with those people that were sent to help me enter the spirit world or go on to continue to live life. I had chosen life. God must have bigger plans for me or I would have died. I do not know his plan for me, but am sure he will reveal it as time goes on. I now know dying is not the end, it is only the beginning. This experience has also brought me closer to God/Jesus and family. I do believe in angels.

I do not believe angels are the figure people envision in their thoughts of people with long flowing hair, beautiful white gowns and wings. By definition, an angel means "messengers of God." If one is helping another, then you are doing God's work and are indeed a messenger of God. Angels walk the earth everywhere and all of us can see them if we really look. We ourselves are sometimes angels or could be an angel, a messenger of God. The person on a corner trying to get a few pennies to survive, the homeless person, the refugee, the child that does not have a Christmas present or toys to play with, the neighbour that needs a helping hand occasionally. Just open your eyes and look — really look — and you will see angels all around you, and opportunities to do the work of God. LOOK! Even you can be and are. Say a kind word to somebody, help a person in need, and it really is not that hard. There's no need to fly thousands of miles to help people in some far away village; people in need are all around you.

I relate to the following story: there were a bunch of mosquito larva on the surface of a small pond, a bog really. These larvae wondered why the larvae that got the urge and climbed the blade of grass never came back. These larvae decided when they got the urge to climb the blade of grass they would come back and tell the others what was up there, what they saw — share the information, so to speak. In time, eventually all the larva individually got the urge to climb the blade of grass. They climbed it and as they neared the top, their wings sprouted out and they could fly. They soon understood why others did not return: the world they saw and that they were now a part of was so beautiful, they just wanted to stay and explore with many of their friends that shared the space on the pond with them. They did not want to return to the pond because this world was so beautiful that they decided to stay and explore it. To enjoy their old friends' company seemed important because they knew all the others would also join them one day soon. I really appreciate and know the importance of both God and family in my life.

In the early days of the ABI recovery I noted that my left eye was still closed. I could not open it and even when I forced it open I had blurred and triple vision. Worrisome indeed. Doctors told me this would be OK in a few weeks. Over the next few days I would look out the window and do some self-talk. I looked out over the city through the hospital windows and said this is where I will be going back home, so I am getting better now and my eye is healed. One day the doctor gave me an eye patch to place over my good eye, he said that would force my closed eye to open. Yes, when I placed the patch over my good eye, my closed eye would open. I was retraining my left eye to open. Over the next few weeks, my closed eye gradually opened fully.

Every day Stefan and Nancy came to visit. They came to spend as much time as they could with me. Suzanne did not come to visit every day, she could not because she had a young child and was unable to spend a lot of time at hospital but did the best she could. Stefan would often take me for a walk every evening around the hospital ward hallway that was in a square pattern. This really helped my recovery. Nancy and I also went walking during her visits to the hospital.

After my family left for the day, the nights are a lonely time in the hospital. I think I had PTSD after my brain injury. I was in a semi-private room, but I really needed a private room. Due to many government healthcare cuts and bed closures, none were available. Government folks cut most things except their own pay and pensions. When the patient in my room in the bed next to me would be released, another emergency patient would be brought in late at night to fill the bed. I could hear doctors and nurses working on the person, and this caused me much anxiety with lack of sleep and the rest that I needed greatly.

In the QEII hospital, I really disliked and felt embarrassed each morning because I had to take a shower with a fully clothed nurse in my bathroom monitoring/watching me. I realized I had to check my dignity at the door when arriving at hospital. I remember saying to nurses it was not fair that I had to take my clothes off while she was fully dressed. Guess I was returning to normal. Nurses were watching me to understand if I was recovering to perform tasks normally — to ensure my brain was recovering to work properly. She was a cutie and very sweet woman though. I am sure this was a job she did not particularly enjoy, but a necessary part of it. Eventually I did get to shower alone as I recovered.

Due to the ABI I had acquired a habit of fixating on things. One night I was watching a documentary on CNN about John the Baptist. All night I could not sleep because I kept thinking and asking myself the same question over and over again: Why did John the Baptist exist? At approximately 6 A.M. the next morning, I remembered what was said in my high school Grade 11 Literature classes when we studied Homer's "Iliad": "We the gods will live as long as humans believe in us." Centuries ago the Greek gods were prayed to and worshipped by many people. Centuries later they are not part of any belief anymore, they are only legends, and my conclusion was: John the Baptist exists because we believe he did. With my brain injury I was Ok with that answer. I then got some much-needed sleep. I wish I had remembered the greatest book ever written, the Bible, also tells us about John the Baptist.

I had many bad days in hospital but always tried to stay positive. Today I am told I am sometimes a pessimist.

"I am not a pessimist, just an experienced optimist," I say.

The books I read, such as "The Power of the Subconscious Mind" by Joseph Murphy, I remembered and reread it. I put it to work for me, and also prayed to God and the Madonna Virgin Mary when I was feeling good and not so good. I remember I had opportunity to visit many Catholic churches and shrines in Italy. The one that made the most impression on me was The Shrine of The Virgin of the Rosary of Pompeii. Many miracles have taken place at this place. I invite you to look it up on the Internet or even visit. It is an amazing place. The times I prayed, a peace and calm came over me like I was being hugged. I think Jesus was saying, "I have you and all is OK."

A man told me once he was searching for God. I replied that I did not know God was lost.

"You and I may have been lost on many occasions," I said to him, "but God has never been. He is only a prayer away. Close your eyes, whisper a prayer and there he is. Feel it, embrace it. As humans, we are made in the image of God so if you want to see what God looks like just look in the mirror. We may not think we are God or look like God, but the bible says we are made in his image. We can be God-like if we so choose to be. It really is your choice. Do the best you can, sometimes do even better than that. All humans are born with two dogs inside. One is the dog of hate, prejudice, envy, greed, narcissism, malice and pride. The other is the dog of love, faith, charity and empathy. When those two dogs fight inside you, the winner will be the dog you feed. You can choose to feed the dog of love, faith, charity and empathy every hour of every day. God has given us free choice. The dog you feed is your choice."

I remember the hospital was so cold at night. I felt so cold and was shivering all night long. Maybe it was due to the blood thinners. My family would cover me with heated blankets and in later days brought a handmade quilt made by some woman in Cape Breton, Nova Scotia. I had it at my own place in my linen closet. The quilt was given to me by an old flame in Sydney, Cape Breton, Nova Scotia, Canada. It was so warm and improved my rest substantially. I have had this quilt for years and not used it very much, now it would go to good use. I still have that quilt today.

On a really positive note, one evening while talking to my girlfriend, Nancy, who was not my fiancé yet, I told her she needed to get a band. She asked what type of band and what for. I said to her that I had a diamond in my safe at home. I had bought this diamond two years earlier when I was home and healthy and was thinking maybe I would want to get married again sometime. I thought diamonds were not getting any cheaper so buying one now to keep made sense, besides it was a positive I was sending out into the universe. I purchased it and placed it in my home safe until I felt the time was right. It was a single diamond, not a ring. My thought was the woman I gave it to could decide on the setting for it. I would get the diamond placed in the setting she chose, buy that setting before placing it on her finger.

"Are you proposing to me?" she asked.

"I guess I am," I said.

She accepted, but one problem I said, was that I do not remember the combination to my safe. On the day I proposed, apparently the nurses were having a bad day. When they heard the news all were so happy, and they said it really helped to hear such good news on such a bad day. Later, I remembered I had the combination numbers in my wallet. I asked Nancy to get the diamond and to pick out a setting that she liked and I would pay for it. Anyway, the long and short of it is she accepted my proposal. She got the diamond from my safe and she loved it. What woman would not like a 3.5 carat Canadian Ice diamond (plus the setting and the band)? Nancy made an appointment with a jeweler and she found the most beautiful setting one could imagine. One day in hospital I was not having a great day, feeling poorly indeed. I had talked to Nancy who was on way to her appointment with the jeweller. I told her Suzanne was visiting and was with me, I will be OK. Later in the day my cell phone rang. It was Nancy. "Honey, I am at the jeweller and you have to give me a budget for the ring setting."

"Have you found something?" I asked.

"I have," she said. "I will pass the phone over to the jeweller and he will explain," she said.

The jeweler described to me the setting and the price and all I said was give her what she wants. Nancy and the lady at the jewelry counter, whom Nancy had told our story to, both started to cry. The ring would now be five carats including the setting, but worth every cent. It was for Nancy, after all.

Out on a weekend pass a few weeks later we went to pick up the ring. It was beautiful. Nancy and the jeweller did such a great job. It was the fourth or fifth weekend in hospital and my family got me released for the afternoon on a Sunday. Nancy and my son had secured a wheelchair on loan for me to use if I needed it because I was still weak and unsteady. I remember getting on the elevator and descending to the lower floors, I had not been on an elevator since the ABI. The feeling in my head was really weird and a little scary as we descended. On the drive home — Nancy was driving (the doctor had told me not drive for at least 6 months) — looking through the windshield, all the sights coming at me were overwhelming. They caused a weird sensation on my left frontal brain lobe (where I had the stroke). I had to close my eyes because my brain was having trouble processing the information, and it was hardly bearable. I had not been advised of this while in hospital. When I went home I purchased dark sunglasses, which I would wear often over the months ahead when in a moving car. I also found they helped when I was in a grocery store because they drowned out the bright lights that stressed my brain.

# CHAPTER TWENTY-TWO

After a few weeks at the QE II, the doctors were trying to get me admitted to the rehab centre but no beds were available, so I had to wait. Another downside of the public health care system is the waiting periods. This set my recovery back some, I think. The QE II was not equipped for rehabilitation but were doing the best they could. In April 2015, I was advised a bed at rehab was available. My family was very happy, as was I. In April, I was transferred to the Nova Scotia Rehabilitation Centre via an ambulance. They were going to move me while I was lying in my bed but I refused. I walked to the ambulance and then sat in a wheelchair for my move, arriving at the Nova Scotia rehab centre with Nancy at my side. I was standing/walking as best I could.

I was advised by the Admitting nurse that only a private room was available. My Blue Cross Insurance only covered semi-private. I would have to take this room, as it was the only room available or I would have to leave. The Public system I thought! So, I had to take it but Suzanne made the deal that I would not have to pay for a private room. That was great considering I was now without any income due to the ABI. I would have to rely on my savings and family for the foreseeable future.

This room really helped me feel better than the QE II semi-private room I had been in for some weeks. I was soon set up with a Physiotherapy (PT) and Occupational Therapy (OT) schedule. I always say that I felt better the day I went into rehab than when I came out of rehab. It seemed rehab was about checking boxes, one program fits all. Check the boxes get me home and out of the public system ASAP. The programs were designed for people in worse condition than I was, but it was what they said I needed to do. I thought I would get assessed and a program set up for me based on my condition. The rehab programs are not tailored to the individual needs based, on his or her condition, or issues. It is what it is. This is what you have to do because it is the program. The Public system is not always made to suit your needs. Do not depend on the medical community for solutions. They have lots of information, they can patch you up to send you home, but you have to find your own solutions. Over the months ahead when I was released to go home most, the solutions I found that helped me the most were those I found by accident or by talking to previous stroke victims who have recovered their lives.

At rehab I read a lot. In 1986, I was introduced to books written by Leo Buscaglia: "Loving and Learning",

"Parenthood and Living", and also "The Way of the Bull." I was hooked, and I re-read those books. During my stay in rehab I enjoyed reading many types of books, like Eckhart Tolls' "The Power of Now" and "Awakening Your Life's Purpose." Also, books by Don Miguel Ruiz: "The Four Agreements" and "The fifth agreement." These books have helped shape my life. No book changed my life more than one written by Joseph Murphy's "The Power of the Subconscious Mind.". I recommend it to all for a great read and put it to work for you. My most recent reading experience was "The Red Notice." Wow what a book, I hope it will be a movie. I also read "Irving vs Irving", which was a disappointing book. The writer spent a lot of writing trying not to ruffle any Irving feathers. The Irving's are a rich and powerful family in the province New Brunswick, and are very politically connected in Canada.

One good thing about rehab was I would be able to go home with family on weekends, if I wanted to. Soon I was requesting a weekend pass. It was my first weekend to go home on weekend pass and I looked forward to it so much. I stayed at Nancy's place and when we got up on Saturday morning I wanted go for a walk, and of course Nancy went along also. It was a good walk and I felt good. I did not realize it may lead to fatigue — a common side effect for those with early brain injury recovery. On Sunday, I wanted to go with my granddaughter to the wildlife park. We did go, along with Suzanne, Nancy and little Charlotte. We also planned a picnic. After we arrived I went down into the park with my family; I really wanted to see Charlotte enjoy the animals. After a short time walking, I was feeling really tired and said I am going back to the car. They asked if I could get back ok. "I will be fine," I said. I left to walk back alone and just made it back. My legs and body was feeling really tired and I fell into the car seat to rest. Wow, I was thinking, I am not normal yet. I was a little afraid of how I felt, and had anxiety. I got myself calmed down and fell asleep for a short nap. Soon the group returned and we left for home. Arriving home I lay down to rest and soon asked Nancy to take me back to rehab where she got me all settled into bed. I was tired and not feeling great. Nancy informed the nurses of my condition. They checked my Blood Pressure which was o.k. at the time. I got up early the next morning, had a shower, then thought I would do some work on my laptop. Soon I started to feel sweaty and my legs were aching. I was feeling like I had no energy. I did not know at the time what it was, but I later realized it was the onset of severe fatigue. I've never felt this way ever before in my life. Later that day, Stefan came to visit. I asked him to go down to the first floor to go outside for a while, so we did. Shortly after getting outside I began to feel not so good and asked him to take me back to my room, so he did. As I was getting back into bed I told him I felt like I was going to pass out, he should go get the nurse. He went to talk to a nurse and also called Nancy. The nurse came and she soon realized I was having difficulty. She checked my BP and would not say what the reading was. Apparently, it was very high. After consulting the doctor (if this was a private system, a doctor would have been available in the hospital in minutes, but the public system is so lacking in good health care) by phone the nurse introduced a nitro patch to help get my BP down. The nurse stayed with me for some time, monitoring my BP and talking to me. I was having anxiety. Anxiety is not good for high BP. The nurse did the best she could to calm me down. Nancy also arrived and I always felt better when she was near. Sometime before midnight I asked Stefan and Nancy to go home to get some rest, they needed it. I wanted them near but could not be too selfish, after all they had jobs to attend next day. They wanted to stay, but I said I would be o.k. and would call them in the morning. They did leave. I was scared but happy for them to get rest. The Head Nurses gave orders to the Night Nurses to monitor my BP every hour. I would hear them coming every hour over the night — a long night for me. I slept very little, waking up if asleep for BP check, but did manage to fall to sleep occasionally. At 6:30 A.M. my BP was back to an acceptable level, and the nurse said she would leave you me alone for a while to get some sleep but would come by to check on me. Over the next week or two my BP was to be monitored/checked at least 5 times a day, doctors' orders. It got to the point where when I heard the nurse coming with the BP machine I got anxious. Especially at night. I had myself convinced there was something wrong and that I was not being told all my health issues. In a hospital alone for many hours a day your thoughts run over time and convince you of many things that are not real

The next day I stayed in bed all day. The doctor's conclusion was I had over done it on the weekend out, and was in a state of severe fatigue that could last for days. My BP meds were increased and a 10mg was added for my anxiety. I was told the Celexa would take a week to actually be of use. During the next two weeks I had severe anxiety often, too often, it really bothered me. All of this sort of brought my BP under control. I was scheduled to be released in late May. The week in May prior to my scheduled release, I had fatigue again and my BP increased again. A nitro patch was stuck onto my chest and that week was a rough one for me health wise, physically and mentally. My legs were now causing trouble, pain and stiffness every day. This leg pain would continue for many months ahead, long after release from hospital. It has been more than two years now and my legs are just starting to feel better. They have been stiff and aching every day I get up. As of just a few weeks ago, doctors now think it is not neurological but something else. They have no answers — fact is they have no idea and are not trying to find the answer. They never do, it seems. I soon realized if I am to recover I will have to become my own life support system, find my own solutions.

Every morning while at rehab a doctor came to visit. I would talk to the doctors, who heard me but did not listen to me — especially about my leg pain. They did not try to find the cause, they just added Tylenol Arthritis 24-hour release to my meds. This helped some on the first day I started to take it. Nancy and Stefan were visiting and I did play a little guitar. Playing guitar was a worry but may be a good therapy. I had noticed a few days earlier I could not make some guitar chords with my left hand. My left arm, hand and left leg were most affected by the stroke. I even laughed and joked that evening, and this made Nancy and Stefan feel much better. I was not a great guitar player. I had jokingly asked my neurosurgeon week's earlier if could now play guitar again, and he answered, "Yes, you can. It would be good to help your recovery."

"Well good, because I could not play it before."

In days ahead I was finding the Tylenol were not doing much anymore. The doctors had no solution as usual, and this caused me worry. I began to check out the side-effects to the meds. I noted the worst leg pain started after doctors increased my BP morning meds (Perindopril doubled from a 5mg to a 10mg tablet). I discussed this with the doctor who said she had not heard of that before and seemed to not believe me. She decided to increase my evening dose of a different type of BP pill and lower the morning dose. Soon after the reduction of the morning dose from 10mg to 4mg, the worst of my leg pain subsided a little to be more bearable. **Amazing!!**

Worth noting here is that I was having some noticeable cognitive issues, My memory seemed to be doing well, better than expected, but I had lots of anxiety like PTSD, cognitive fatigue, brain fog. My laptop was very frustrating to me, anything electronic was difficult. I was unable perform at my pre-stroke level, I was slower moving, my brain was slower understanding things, and I fixated on things — especially thoughts. One night I asked a nurse a medical question and she said she did not know the answer. All night I could not sleep because I was thinking I was in hospital with a nurse that did not know answers. It kept me awake at night and afraid to sleep. One must be careful how you answer a person with a brain injury. I suffered from:

1. Chronic Fatigue
2. Unable to think clearly
3. Brain fog
4. Irritability
5. Muscle weakness
6. Did not cope well with being alone
7. Anxiety
8. Tiredness and fatigue
9. Attention Deficit
10. Unable to multi task
11. Confusion at times
12. Unable to use a computer properly
13. Lack of full use of my left hand
14. I really had to concentrate to get my left hand to do what I wanted it to do
15. Difficulty typing on my laptop even today. This has been a real obstacle to me writing this book but I have persevered despite it all
16. double vision that lasted for almost two months
17. Impaired fine motor skills

18. Unable to stand in place very long
19. Impaired balance
20. Unable to return to work. This bothers me even today because I want to get back to normal
21. Slower moving
22. Unclear thinking
23. Lack of coordination for swimming — I could swim before the stroke
24. Lack of motivation is very common among brain injury survivors, and one negative word can discourage.

A typical day for me at the Nova Scotia rehab facility: wake at 7 A.M., shower/shave.

At 8 A.M. breakfast if on time, not most days, a little rest. Then at 9 A.M. I would go down to the ground level to get outside for some air and maybe get a decaf coffee at the cafeteria if it was open. After coffee, go back to bed to rest a while. At 11 A.M. I had a scheduled Occupational Therapy session. Many of these sessions were cancelled for reasons such as the therapist had another meeting scheduled, was out sick, etc. It seems nurses in the Public system have a lot of sick days. At Noon, lunch, but it was never on time and always cold even if it was supposed to be a hot lunch. It was served in a dining room with all other inmates present. After lunch I had a rest period, then at 2 P.M. Physiotherapy (PT). After PT, I usually stopped at Recreational Therapy for a group decaf coffee or cards and chat. At 5 P.M. we had dinner. It was never much to look forward to and I very seldom ate it. Many evenings, the family brought in something for me. They were worried because I had lost so much weight. I went from 190 lbs to 145 lbs, and they wanted me to eat to help regain my strength.

After dinner Nancy and Stefan would visit. Sometimes Nancy came to visit in the afternoon and Stefan came in the evening. They did shifts, it seemed. Some evenings when I was not feeling well, having anxiety, Nancy would lay in bed next to me. This always calmed me down and I also felt better. She was a real Florence Nightingale. When she visited, we talked about nothing and everything. On some days, Suzanne came to visit with Charlotte. I would hear Charlotte coming running down the hall saying "Where is Papa Momma?" She would look in my door and I could hear her giggle. She brought a smile to my face and my made heart happy.

"Hi Papa!" she would say, then get up on my bed with a little help from mom. I loved those visits. I know a grandparent's love for a grandchild is unmatched by any other. She would say "Walk Papa." I would get out of bed, and with her hand in mine we would walk the hallways. Those were beautiful moments. I felt so good and so proud in those moments, great memories were made. Even when times are not the best, make the best of the time you have.

> **I read a quote once, as I remember it goes something like this:**
>
> *"Life is not about the time you spend but how you spend the time you have."*

I recommend be kind to yourself, be good to your family and spend quality time with them. They are your biggest and best asset. At work in most cases you are only an employee number, your family and your God knows you by name, and have concern about your happiness and health. God wants you to be your best self. He wants the best for you, just have faith. When the chips are down, your family are the ones who you need and will be there for you. I know from experience. Most people go a whole lifetime and not realize this. The earlier in life you realize this the better life will be for you and your family.

# CHAPTER TWENTY-THREE

As my release from hospital neared, some decisions were necessary, like where I would live. I had my own place but could I live alone and care for myself properly? Did I need 24-hour care? There were discussions with doctors, and my son, daughter and Nancy. This caused us all much stress and anxiety. In late June, a week before release, I was thinking a lot about going home. Going home thoughts gave me some anxiety. I was leaving the safety of the hospital, not going back to my own place, no job, no income, close my small business. How long before I would be able to work again? What does my recovery look like? How am I going to get through this? My life had changed drastically. I had many anxious days and scary thoughts about what to do. What is God's plan for me? I came close to dying but was still living, and God obviously has some more plans for me. Time has a way of figuring things out, I thought.

**I remember a quote from Wayne Dwyer;**

*"We are not humans having a spiritual experience, we are spiritual beings having a human experience."*

Wayne also talked about the synchronicity of life: everything happens for a reason, although even though I was unable to understand why such a thing had happened to me. Even today I have no answer for that, except God has a greater plan for me. I have meditated on this question sometimes but no answer seems come to me. Maybe his plan was for me to write this book.

I had lived alone for the most part since Sharon and I divorced in 2000. I had worked in the Alberta oil sands for four years on contract as a QA specialist, then later in Newfoundland for four years as a QA specialist and as a field engineer for FRP Installations at Vale Newfoundland and Labrador Limited. I was very independent. I had met Nancy about a year prior to the ABI, and her birth parents were Newfoundlanders, but she was born in Halifax and put up for adoption. We hit it out of the park from the start. Nancy had been adopted by a good family in Halifax at a very young age, she had grown up and was schooled there, got married and divorced there also. The decision was made that I would go to stay with Nancy until I was doing better and could move back to my own place. My daughter is member of the Canadian military, the Air Force — and was not home much, or at best had weird shifts and a child at home. Stefan would help the best he could. I could decide to have shared time between Suzanne and Stefan's house. Nancy is self-employed, works from home and could be more flexible. We all agreed this probably was best fit for me, so I went to Nancy's house.

In June, 2015 prior to my release, we had a family meeting with doctors and therapist for post stroke recommendation for my recovery and life at home. I was released form Nova Scotia rehab midday. I was going home, great! I knew I had to find my own solutions for recovery and my family and I would have to be my own life support system. There's no support in Nova Scotia or Canada for brain injury survivors after hospital release, they are left to fend for themselves. Our Public health care system has really failed brain injury survivors.

At Nancy's I soon created a schedule for exercise to help fill up my day. A typical day over the next three months — when I was not in the middle of many days of fatigue — was awake and get up approximately 7:30 A.M., then shower and shave. At 8 A.M take meds, have breakfast, then lay down to rest a while. At 9 A.M. get Nancy's Sheltie dog, Flash, ready and head out for our walk. Walking was really slow the first few weeks. Each week I set a goal of how far I could walk and return safely. At the end of each week I would walk a little further and that would be the walk for Flash and I, for the next week. I would return from the daily walks, then rest and watch television, read etc. At noon I made lunch. After lunch, I was off to bed for a nap. At 2 P.M. I'd get up and get Flash ready for our afternoon walk. Back from the walk, I'd rest (my legs always were hurting every day with pain and stiffness. How long would this last? I asked every day), but Flash and I soldiered on every day. Some days I got tired and slowed as if I had enough. Flash sensed I needed to go further to finish my goal of distance to walk some days, and she would get behind me then nudge her nose against the back of my leg as if to cheer me on saying, "I know you can do it. Come on a little further, you can do it." Flash was a real caring friend indeed. I think she looked forward to the walk more then I. Flash gave me the courage to say, "I will try again tomorrow." If I did not get up early enough she would start to bark as if to remind me. My legs were aching and stiff every day, they bothered me a lot, but I needed to keep going — it was crucial to my recovery. I was not feeling very strong because I had lost a lot of my strength and muscle. I felt tired most of the time. I also had cognitive fatigue, and felt frustrated and impatient. I was not allowed to drive so could not go anywhere, not even to run an errand. Although I had purchased a 2015 Audi Q5 SUV just a month or so prior to the ABI, it had been parked in the underground garage of my apartment building ever since. Nancy checked on it occasionally. I often wondered, when or if I would ever get to drive myself again. How long would recovery take? As my son said, "As long as it takes." Sometimes I wished I could skip a year or more, whatever was necessary to bring me to a time when I would be feeling better, but now I look back and realize I have learned a lot over the past two years.

> **I like the following quote by Lance Armstrong:**
>
> *"Pain is temporary. It may last a minute, an hour, or a day or a year, but eventually it will subside and something else will its place. If I quit, however, it lasts forever."*

I was not going to quit. I have no quit in me. I am going to recover and I will make it.

Just a few weeks after release from hospital I received a call from the Acquired Brain Injury (ABI) team to set up a visit. There were three women that would visit me many times over the next three months. They were Lynn, a specialist in Occupational Therapy; Ronda, a Recreational Therapist; and Ainsley, a Social Worker. They were helpful in my recovery. Lynn noted I was having trouble with my vision, especially the peripheral vision. My brain was having an issue processing all the information that was coming into it, therefore helping increase my fatigue. She also noted I was not seeing items or things that were in my peripheral vision properly (i.e.: if somebody approached from the side I was not noticing them or seeing as soon as I should). To help fix this she brought me a pair of glasses that had the outside part of side of the lenses shaded over. This helped refocus my eyes forward and improved my peripheral vision. I do not know how, but this really helped over the next few weeks. I wore those when out on walks and around the house as much as possible. I looked a little geeky for sure but I did not care, I was so past that.

Ronda was fixated on getting me to go take buses around the city. I was not interested in that, besides I told her "By the end of September I will be driving again." She also suggested I join a gym. I did eventually but not that summer — I was not ready. I did join the Canada Games Centre when I felt ready to do it.

At Nancy's during the summer I had many bouts with fatigue. I began to get interested in the side effects of the pills I was taking, so I researched for that information. I noted the 5 P.M. pill of 10mg of Amlodipine for BP, that one side effect stated was fatigue. I then talked to my GP about if this could be enhancing my fatigue bouts and could we possibly lower that dose. I had been checking my BP regularly and recording it for his review. He had also been monitoring my BP during my visits to see him. He agreed and lowered my dose to 5mg, but I had to check my BP at 8 AM., 12 P.M., 5 P.M. and 8 P.M. I had to record it and let him review, and also if my BP was elevated to a certain point I was to call him immediately. Taking 5mg did not make any difference to my BP level, which was a good sign indeed.

Soon after release from rehab, all my family and I were off to the White Point Resort on Nova Scotia's south shore. In early March, a couple of weeks before the stroke, I had booked a four-day getaway at there for Father's day weekend for Nancy and I. As my hospital release grew nearer I told Nancy I wanted also to invite my kids and granddaughter, to which she agreed. This would also give Suzanne, Stefan and Charlotte a chance to spend some time together with each other and us, after this most difficult spring of health issues for me. I was going! We were going! We all needed a break, we decided. Nancy would drive my new SUV and we would leave Friday mid-morning.

Stefan would drive with Suzanne and Charlotte later after work on Friday. Nancy and I left about mid-morning on the Friday, stopping at a fruit and veggie stand along the way and then the Superstore in Liverpool for some groceries. I noted I was feeling cranky and frustrated, probably due to my ABI. Arriving at the store, Nancy and I went inside. We argued in the store for nothing of any importance, as most arguments are. We were both upset, no doubt due to the frustration and worry we had gone through these past months. Arriving at White Point we got ourselves settled away. Easy decisions about dinner and sleeping arrangements needed to be made before my kids arrived. This was a beautiful place, with our cottage just a few yards from the beach, and ocean. We could hear the rolling of the surf inside the cottage. It had a fireplace, a wall of natural forming rocks between us and the sandy beach to which we had good access. My mobile rang and it was the kids saying they were not far away. Nancy and I immediately left for Liverpool to get pizza for dinner and were back when the kids arrived. It was a sunny, warm afternoon and all were feeling great about the weekend to come. Sharing with family, this was the thing to do. Surf, sandy beach, food, soda and beer or wine, and milk for Charlotte. No alcohol for me, doctors' orders. I had no issue with not drinking alcohol as I never did drink much at any time in my life. It was a great start to our weekend. Charlotte loved the outside and the freedom of being able to roam around. She just fell in love with the rabbits that came and went at will, it seemed. Uncle Stefan was spending so much time with her, just what they needed. Charlotte sensed I was not well she always came to show me something she had found or ask me to come look at something. It was a great evening walking the beach, relaxing and talking about the past months' stresses and other things that came up as do when in conversation. Nancy and my kids were having some drinks and relaxing. They deserved this, I thought. At about 11 P.M. all were off to bed and falling asleep with the sounds of the ocean waves pounding on the sea shore. I woke twice during the night but snuggled Nancy and fell back to sleep with the music of the waves pounding the beach. It felt like home. She looked so beautiful in the moonlight shining through the window. She gave the moon a reason to shine, I thought. Wow! It's wonderful and just what we all needed and deserve. I felt happy and content in these moments and grateful I had made the plans.

Saturday morning, I was up at 7:30 A.M. to make my breakfast and take my meds. Soon Charlotte woke and was up and about, so everyone got out of bed. We had planned shower times for all the previous evening. After all there was just one bathroom. The persons with a number 1 or 2 issue got bathroom access first, showers later, depending on the planned time. After breakfast Charlotte immediately went outside with Stefan to feed the rabbits. At about 10 A.M. I asked Nancy to go for a walk as I did every morning at home.

We went, but it was a little hilly for me — I still found hills hard on my legs. After the walk, we noted that Suzanne and Stefan were at the beach with Charlotte having some fun. Nancy and I got beach-ready and went to join them. Just after arriving at the beach I became aware that I was feeling tired so decided to go back to the cottage to lay down. Fatigue was setting in. I lay around most of the day hoping to be feeling great for the Father's Day family breakfast we had planned at the resort lodge dining room on Sunday morning. On Sunday morning, I was still feeling somewhat fatigued but tried to not spoil the day for us as a family. Although I was not feeling great I said I was OK, and off we went to breakfast. At the lodge we found a table and ordered breakfast. Before breakfast was served I began to cry, saying I was sorry but I had to go back to bed. I was not feeling great, and my emotional control had been a problem since I had the stroke, plus I so wanted to have a good weekend and be part of the Father's Day family breakfast. I went back to the lodge, and soon after Stefan came with my breakfast. He talked to me and consoled me, knowing I was upset and fatigued. The kids had to leave to go home mid-afternoon Sunday, for work Monday morning. Nancy and I would stay the one more night alone. In the afternoon, we lit a fire in the fireplace. It was raining hard and windy. The surf was rough. We were really cozy in our cottage, so we pulled out the couch into a bed and watched a movie. We could also hear the rain, wind and waves. I was really tired so we lay around the rest of the day. I really wish it was a better weekend for us all but a stroke survivor has extended health recovery time needed. One has to be patient and resilient, this I know. Every day was a challenge. It is hard to get up, get going and try to stay positive. It is still that way over two years later.

After returning home, I fell into a bad bout of fatigue for eight days. I was mostly just laying around on a bed or couch and sleeping, reading and watching TV. It was not good. I felt so lousy. I said to all we will go again next year and it will be better.

We did go again in June 2016 and it was better. A great Father's Day weekend indeed. One of the highlights, maybe the most important memorable highlight of the weekend for me, was the moments Nancy, me, Charlotte, Suzanne, Stefan and his girlfriend, Maggie, were all walking down the sandy beach with the surf waves rolling in just nipping at our bare feet then receding back to the safety of the large ocean. All of us were holding hands as a family: Nancy and I were holding hands, Charlotte was between Suzanne and I holding our hand. As we walked, Charlotte began to sing the songs from her favourite movie "Frozen." On occasion, she let go of our hands, looked toward the sky and sang at the top of her lungs, her voice rising in the song parts that required it just like in the movie. With arms open and directed upward, she made theatrical gestures and sometimes twirled around in the sand. So beautiful. When she finished singing each song we all applauded and cheered her on like any family would in those special moments. Just awesome, wow! That night, as her mom was tucking her into bed after lots of goodnight kisses from all of us, Charlotte said to her mom, "I feel so happy. I think happy comes from inside because my heart feels so happy, all my family are here." Wow! This nearly three-year-old child just expressed something that takes most people a lifetime to learn. Family is important. Threading the happy family needle of life.

During my first few months at Nancy's, she noticed I was interrupting people when they were talking. I could not wait to say what I needed to say and sometimes it had nothing to do with the conversation at hand. I was easily distracted and found it difficult to control emotions. I was crying for almost no reason. Sometimes I did not have much of a filter on what I would say, probably due to my crankiness. I did not worry about or think about others' feelings or care what others thought. Sitting in a group of people was almost impossible. It was and is difficult to follow more than one conversation or person speaking at a time. A person speaking fast was and is annoying and difficult for me to follow. Nancy's daughters speak very fast, and when they were talking it really annoyed me and made me cranky; it was the brain injury. I was annoyed I could not keep up with the fast talking, it really fatigued my brain quickly and made me very cranky. I just glazed over and tuned them out. It annoyed me so I just gave up and started having my own internal conversation and thoughts. Being a Newfoundlander people talking fast is a normal way of conversation for Newfoundlanders; we speak fast because we think faster than most other Canadians, but now that fast speaking really bothered me.

Also over the summer I was soon feeling a little better and able to do more without getting fatigued. The bouts with fatigue lessened and my cognitive and physical strength improved. It just required patience and perseverance, prayers, faith in God and in myself. I also learned to take time outs when I got confused or cranky, and this really helped.

**My Sheltie friend, Flash**

# CHAPTER TWENTY-FOUR

Late in July 2015, while at home after a midday nap I noted that I was having double vision in my left eye. I went to look in the mirror to review how I was seeing. I was alone in the house and was scared of a possible on-coming stroke again. I dialed Nancy's mobile but she was out with a client. We talked a short time then she said she would head home. While waiting for her I lay on the couch hoping this would pass but it continued. I was not panicking. Nancy arrived and we soon headed out to the QE II Emerge. At Emerge intake we informed the clerk of my problem and noted to her that I had a stroke a few months before, and had spent some time in that hospital recovering from it. The clerk fast tracked us for a doctor checkup and review. Soon I was seeing a doctor and was on my way for a C-Scan. The C-scan was the regular type. Soon I was back in the emerge room seeing the doctor again. He was checking my strength, reflexes and vision, plus asking me many questions. The doctor said the C-scan results were a little concerning and wanted me to have another type that required a dye to be injected. So back to the C-scan I went intravenous was hooked to my arm and a dye injected. I had this done before and did not have any fear or anxiety. When the dye was injected a person can feel the warm fluid trailing through the body — a really weird feeling — and also feel pressure to go to the bathroom to urinate, but I knew what to expect. It went well, and I was soon back in the Emergency Room with the nurse and doctor. I went through all the checks the doctor thought necessary, but nothing I had not had done before. First, the doctor thought I may have had a minor stroke. By this time my vision had returned to normal, which was a good sign indeed. The doctor soon left and a nurse was assigned to monitor me while we waited for the new C-scan results. The nurse told us my BP was elevated but not to a point requiring any extra concern. I was lying on the bed and waiting for the C-scan results. The doctor soon returned with the results and advised us they were negative. That was great news, excellent, and a sigh of relief. The doctor said I had had a silent headache but there is a more technical name for it. It is common and can cause vision issues.

"Great, so let's go home" I said to Nancy.

"No, not yet," the doctor said.

I was given a prescription to replace the daily Aspirin with Clopdogrel Bisulfate (Plavix). I was given six tablets to take immediately and then to wait 30 minutes before we went home, none the worse for the little scare. I continue to take the Plavix every day in morning, which continues up to today and will for the future. There were some calls from my kids and siblings about the little scare. The next day I was in a full-blown fatigue that would last for seven days. I really disliked the way I felt when I was in fatigue. "This too will pass, it always does," I said to myself as I settled for a sleep. The fatigue is like the whole body has no energy, even to go to the bathroom or to breathe properly, and the full body aches. Zero energy. As I understand it, the area of my brain that stores the energy I need to use for activities is used up and I have non left. My injured brain not produce the energy as I needed it. The other part of my brain that stores energy for use in breathing, heart beat and other body functions will not let you use that energy. It is needed to keep you alive. I just know the fatigue is a horrible and somewhat scary feeling, but you need to stay calm so you don't use your energy on fear. It is a difficult task to stay calm.

I have to admit that it has been really hard to understand why I've had these health challenges at this time of my life, just a few years before retirement, but I am here. I survived a stroke and brain surgery, and many do not. I am a miracle, God is not done with me yet. I am alive because he has an unfinished plan for me, or just maybe this is his plan for me. I have to move on, we have to move on. It is a waste of time to say "What if?" The word "if" — as stated in a Roger Whitaker song: "If is an illusion, If does not mean anything. Only what really is, is what really counts."

Do not let hurtful things live in your head for free, no use in it. The only purpose it has, is to cloud our view of the goodness of the present. It keeps you from enjoying the present moments you have the way you can and should. When you are angry at somebody for what could eventually be months or years, that person or thing is controlling your life and will until you let it go. Let it go. Sometimes folks do not let things go because it keeps them in what they think is a comfortable place. They have been angry so long, letting that go is a scary thought. You have a right to enjoy all the moments you are alive.

> **As Morgan Freeman stated in the movie "The Shawshank Redemption":**
>
> *"Get busy living or get busy dying."*

The choice is yours. Get going, if you want to live your life. Hanging on to anger and bitterness leads to a wasted life. Changing your thoughts will change your life. Do not get to the point of death and realize you did not live. That would be sad indeed. Get going; there's no time like the present. Forgive, move on, enjoy the days you have left on this earth!!! How you choose to do that is up to you.

# CHAPTER TWENTY-FIVE

In late 2015, I became a member of The Brain Injury Association of Nova Scotia (BIANS), and in June of 2017 I was elected to the board as a survivor representative. This is a volunteer position that allows me to give back to my community, to the people that really need some help, and also get access to good information about my condition or at least where to find such information to help brain injury victims.

The government has forgotten brain injury victims. Brain injury is not always visible by just looking at person. That is good but also a problem because people cannot be convinced of something they cannot see. Many people live with a brain injury and it does not discriminate between male or female, it just happens unexpectedly.

> **The BIANS website states:**
>
> *"One in five sports-related injuries are brain injuries — a concussion is a common brain injury. Approximately one in 26 Canadians are living with a brain injury — stroke is commonly associated with brain injuries. Over 170,000 Canadians incur a brain injury each year. This averages out to about 465 people each day, or about one person every three minutes. An ABI is an injury received to the brain after birth."*

The BIANS website also states the following:

> "Those most at risk for brain injury are youth and young adults. Every year in Canada, over 11,000 people die as a result of a Traumatic Brain Injury. Brain injury is the leading cause of disability and death under the age of 44. It's estimated that over 1.4 million Canadians live with some disability as a result of a brain injury. Many brain injuries are preventable. However, awareness, understanding and prevention are critical to reducing and supporting those affected by brain injury. Please explore the Brain Injury Association of Nova Scotia (BIANS) website and learn more about brain injury and what you could be doing to prevent it."

There are approximately 100,000 people in Nova Scotia who live with brain injury, with approximately 2700 more added each year. Some brain injuries are minor, while others are severe. I personally have met two gentlemen who have become friends. They sit in a wheelchair every day; one cannot walk or talk, and he carries a laminated white sheet of paper with all alphabet letters and numbers from 1 to 10 on it. To have a conversation he points to the letters and numbers to spell words. My other friend lost the ability to walk, read and speak properly. Both men just move from bed to wheelchair, then from wheelchair to their bed to rest or sleep. BIANS membership is free, you just have to call them to sign up. BIANS are not funded by government, money is raised by the organization to self-fund, but it really does need more funding. Brain injury folks really do need a lot of support, but they are not getting it. In Nova Scotia and most of Canada, once a person with brain injury is released from hospital, they are mostly on their own for recovery to find their own solutions to heal, even through all the brain fog. It is difficult for a person without a brain injury, so imagine what it is like for someone who has one. Families and caregivers are very frustrated with the whole system. The Public health care system has failed miserably for brain injury folks, and it seems nobody cares. Only family that are left alone to handle situations as best they can, situations, they are ill-equipped to handle. Some brain injury survivors are left alone because a spouse could not deal with it so has moved on.

# CHAPTER TWENTY-SIX

Staying at Nancy's was not what I thought it would be, or at least how I remember it. Please understand I did not have great brain focus at this time and was really not feeling great. My memory could be a little off about the first few months out of hospital. I think Nancy did the best she could. Her normal day was get up, do her morning routine, then meet with her staff of two, leave to meet clients early morning and then back to the house by mid to late afternoon. I spent a lot of time alone during the summer. Most days I made dinner. Making dinner was not an easy task for me that summer during early recovery, but this was probably a good exercise for me.

I do not think she understood what the road ahead was when I went to her house. She tried her best and did the best she could. Her favourite saying was: "I have to breathe." Her evenings were mostly going for a walk with friends, out to meet someone for coffee or tea. It was probably necessary because of work stress and me having health issues.

Nancy had a needy female friend who was going through a hard time and demanded a lot of her time, but many months later that so-called friend does not call her or return her phone calls. I suppose she has taken all the selfishness she needed. Sometimes friendships are just one-sided for the benefit of one person, just to take everything one can without giving anything back. On many Saturdays or Sundays, Nancy would say "I have to get away" and she would go to meet a friend at a beach for walks and chats. This is the ways it went for the summer and into September. Occasionally we would go for a picnic, depending how I was feeling. Most of the summer it was Flash and I walking on a daily basis until into late autumn. Some days were really lonely, — intense aloneness. I later learned from other ABI folks that the feeling of intense aloneness is a common symptom of an ABI; sometimes it was almost unbearable. Nancy left in late August for a three-week vacation to Africa. Her daughter was working there for a few months so she was off to have some travel with her. This trip was announced to me when I was in rehab and I was not happy to say the least. I was in hospital with life-threatening health issues. Then I thought, well she is not my wife and maybe she should not be in a relationship with me just now. I talked to her about that but she said no she loved me and was planning to stay in our relationship. I am still not convinced at the time this was best for her. Now I think it was probably one of the best things she could have done, she needed some time to spend with her daughter and some relaxation for herself.

# CHAPTER TWENTY-SEVEN

Nancy left for Africa in August 2015. I went to live with my daughter for those three weeks, and I went there the day before Nancy was to leave. The first day at my daughter's was really bad for me. I had lots of anxiety and feelings of aloneness.  I had been and was going through so much, and I had depended on her so much, maybe too much. My BP elevated for the next few days, so I tried to think positive, although it was difficult because I felt abandoned. I called Nancy many times during the first day up until she left, and learned that no matter what, she was going. She had only herself in mind now and maybe she had no choice — maybe she needed to save herself. As time went by I started to think this trip will be good for her and I foolishly thought of ending our relationship before she returned. We had as close a relationship as possible under the circumstances. Today our relationship is not as close as it used to be.

After a few days at my daughters, I settled into a routine and was happy to spend time with her and my granddaughter. It was good for us. During the three weeks at Suzanne's I improved a lot. She was able to change her schedule to get home for lunch and to finish work about mid-afternoon, so I would not be alone too much. I was soon feeling stronger physically and mentally, and my confidence was returning.

During my time with Suzanne, at 7 P.M. after her bath time, Charlotte would say "Papa Mini watch," meaning she wanted us to go watch Mini Mouse. We would go for our special time to watch Mini Mouse on TV in Suzanne's bedroom. At the end of that cartoon they sing a song to which Charlotte would get up and dance on the bed, just moving around and wiggling all over. It was just wonderful, I loved those times, and they were special.

During my time with Suzanne the rehab ABI team came to visit a few times and I appreciated this. The ABI outreach team had started visiting me in the early summer and usually once or twice a week. They were very good at facilitating my return to a somewhat normal life. One down side is, they seemed to want at least one negative thing to report each week.

I maintained contact with Nancy while she was away through Skype and text on her daughter Catlin's phone. This was when she had power and Wi-Fi, which was sporadic at best. Sometimes we went days without contact. I noticed that Suzanne drank protein vegan shakes because she worked out regularly, this helped her muscle recovery she said. I discussed with her the fact my leg muscles were stiff and hurting since mid-May, and maybe that shake would help. She made a shake for me and within three hours my legs were feeling somewhat better. I continued walking daily and drinking a vegan protein shake, and it seemed to help. It also seemed to help lower my fatigue levels. I would continue to have this shake daily for a couple months after that. These shakes also seemed to help me feel stronger. As time grew near for Nancy to return I found myself getting a little excited about it, but I then had the decision of whether I should stay at Suzanne's or go back to Nancy's. Suzanne and Stefan thought I spent too much time alone at Nancy's and maybe I should stay at Suzanne's. I said I would give it some thought. I really enjoyed the evenings, and I started taking my granddaughter downstairs. We would lay on the bed to watch Mini Mouse. This became a routine for us. Stefan and Suzanne thought I was doing better and should stay with Suzanne longer, even after Nancy returned.

I thought it would be best for Nancy and me to spend some time together to try to recover our shattering relationship. We had not had much time to do that since the ABI. I arranged to take a limo to pick her up at the airport. I wanted Charlotte and Suzanne to come also but this did not work out as planned. The limo was not set up to allow a car seat for a child to be fitted. Nancy enjoyed the pickup in the limo and was amazed at how good I was looking and feeling. I soon learned the visit with her oldest daughter was stressful for her. The trip with her daughter went ok.

After Nancy's return, life went back to the same as before she left. In October, I decided maybe some acupuncture may help my leg pain, stiffness and fatigue. Acupuncture on my legs did seem to help, but it also helped drain my bank account. My legs felt better but not completely. My bouts with fatigue were becoming less frequent as the fall wore on.

# CHAPTER TWENTY-EIGHT

*I*n September 2015 I was given the OK to drive again and was very happy. My first few days driving were different but I was moving forward in my recovery. Soon Nancy and I were able to go out for dinner occasionally.  I felt bad about not having a normal life with her. It was obvious she missed that. Sometimes I felt like I was a burden to her. When one was feeling as I had been for months, a romantic dinner was not a thought I had. I was mostly concerned about recovery and how to get feeling better, besides I had no interest in sitting in a restaurant for hours just talking. A side effect of the stroke left me not wanting to engage in long conversations. I could not hold my concentration for that long, and I became bored. I needed to lie down or just close my eyes and rest my brain, but I would do the best I could for Nancy's sake. After I ate I felt like I needed to get out of there but tried my best to stay and talk awhile although it was hard for me. I had to wear a pair of special drummer's ear plugs in a restaurant. They drown out white noise and allow me to hear the people next to me. The noise in restaurants made me tired and agitated, so I was happy to get home and rest.

On October 30, 2015 I returned to my own place, and I was back to living on my own.

In November 2015, I thought it would be nice to arrange a special night out so I purchased tickets for the annual "Ha, Ha, Holiday's" dinner produced by PEG Entertainment, which included three great comedians this year. It was held at the trade and convention centre in downtown Halifax. Nancy thought we should spend the night also so she booked us in at the adjoining Hotel; it was a good idea. We invited friends, and three couples joined us at our table. Nancy and I checked into the Hotel at about 3 P.M. We were worried about my legs and if they would stand up to it, so I brought some Voltaren Extra strength. My legs were aching and feeling stiff so I applied Voltaren about an hour before we went to dinner. This proved to be a big help, as I even got a chance to hold Nancy for a waltz. It was a slow dance and a chance to hold each other, so we loved that. It was a big, emotional step indeed. Both of us had tears in our eyes. Unfortunately, the DJ played mostly all fast songs that evening, which were mostly out of reach for my legs to endure. We stayed until after midnight, which was the latest we had been up for months. We were happy to get into bed that night and were asleep in seconds. The next day my legs were stiff and aching, and I felt a little tired but not bad. I was recovering indeed. Any sign of recovery does give me hope and positive thoughts. "Hurray Moments" I call them.

# CHAPTER TWENTY-NINE

Next was the planning for Christmas. As Christmas came closer I decide to decorate a Christmas tree for Charlotte when she came to visit. Just before Christmas I was watching TV while having dinner and there was a woman showing some palliate exercises, one of which was the importance of stretching the hamstrings. I thought this may help me but my legs are improved a little now so I will wait until after Christmas to try it. I did not want to chance making my legs worse with Christmas almost here. On January 2, I decided that today was the day to stretch the hamstrings. I got a towel, lay on the floor and proceeded, noting not to overdo it. The stretching almost immediately made my legs feel better, especially the upper legs. I continued this exercise for many days to come and it seemed to really help. Another hurray moment.

Later in January, Nancy had an idea about getting into an exercise program at the Canada Games Centre. She investigated this and found it had personal trainers we could possibly work with, so we booked an appointment with one. The guy had certificates for working with people with health issues such a mine. We booked to start the gym on Saturday mornings each week. We used him for a few months but he was really wanting me to do too much — much more than I was able. I would be really stiff and sore the next day, and days following. During the week, I went on my own on Wednesdays, only doing exercises I felt comfortable with. Nancy would go with me when she could. We enjoyed going to the gym together, joked with each other and had fun. We continued this up until March 2016. I continued on at least 2 to 3 times a week without the trainer or her, just doing my own routine alone. I still do it now into 2017, but usually just twice a week. The exercise has helped in my recovery. Today I still have some leg issues but have improved. The important thing is to stay in your wheelhouse and note your stamina as days go, to understand how much exercise is ok for you.

After going to gym, I would drink a vegan protein shake, relax a little and take a hot bath with Epsom salts added to the water. This seems to help a lot. Today it is more than two years after the stroke and subsequent brain surgery, and I am still fighting to get back to good health and strength. It has been a difficult time indeed for me and my family. I think nobody really understands what I have been through. It has been a long, difficult road to recovery, with many frustrations and self-review, and days of feeling blue. It is difficult to stay positive, but being positive is a must, no matter what, along the way. I am not 100% yet — still a ways to go. I just want to feel normal again and I plan to; I look forward to that indeed. I have not been that since March 27, 2015. I have said to lots of people, including my doctor that Newfoundlanders are a resilient and hearty bunch that do not give up easy. It's hard to keep a Newfoundlander down. The important thing is to keep going forward, do not quit. I think we all have fight and resilience in us, we just have to dig down and find it. I have no quit in me. Life has been a struggle since the day I was born. Do not give up. Avoid feeling sorry for yourself and self-loathing. Although sometimes difficult, it is a necessary ingredient in the formula. Your biggest asset is not money or material things, it is your family. It takes some a lifetime to figure that out, some never do. Have I made mistakes in my life? Yes, I have, but remember the past cannot be changed — it is what it is — and so do not spend too much time looking back. It's best to look forward. I repeat to myself many times a day: "I am getting better and better and better every day in every way." I'm training my brain to work positively for me. I know all will be ok for me, and better as time progresses. My family and Nancy sometimes say they want the old me back but I now think the person I was, died in surgery on March 27, 2015, I may never be that guy again, besides I remember that guy could be an asshole sometimes, best to leave him behind maybe.

There is a story I remember about that. I do not know where I heard it or read it. Life is like driving in a car: the rear-view mirrors are small because we should not spend much time looking back or be distracted by it. Life is in front of us, not in the past. Living in the past is to live with regrets.

In the mid fall of 2015, a fellow by the name of Peter came to the house and started to talk about a men's group at Saint Benedict's Catholic Church. The church was just a short walk from the house and he invited me to go. I did go and found this was good for me to be out in a social setting, plus praying and sharing some stories. The setting was non-judgemental, which was great for me under the circumstances. Each Friday morning meeting started with a prayer and a speaker sharing some things about their own life, or how some bible teaching had effected their life for the better. Then in the winter of 2017, Nancy and I attended the Saint Benedict's Alpha program. This program was a very rewarding experience for us. Alpha is an opportunity to explore life and the Christian faith in a friendly, open and informal environment. Alpha is not so much a *course*, but an experience! Gathering once a week over a ten-week period, each Alpha experience brings together people from every walk of life.

# CHAPTER THIRTY

As I continued to recover, in March 2016, Nancy and I discussed a possible vacation. We needed a vacation — she needed one for sure she said — and I thought I was feeling well enough to go. We wanted to return to Hilton Head, South Carolina, and the place where we went on our first trip together. I had surprised her with flights for us to Savannah, Georgia, a car rental and a booking at the Sonesta Resort on Hilton Head Island about an hour's drive away from the airport in Savannah. We had talked about the trip many times during my recovery in hospital. We wanted to return to maybe feel some of that aliveness once again. In March 2016, approximately a year after the stroke, we decided to plan the trip. We would drive and it would be a long road-trip that would take us to a few USA states. I would only drive during the trip as much as I felt up to it, and she would do the bulk of the driving. After all she said she loved to drive. We would stop overnights at hotels, driving no more than eight or nine hours a day. We planned our trip to leave Thursday, April 28, with the first night stopover in Bangor, Maine. We'd spend the second night in Scranton, PA, and a third night in Smithfield, NC. Then we'd be on to Hilton Head, SC, arriving Sunday, May 1. We planned to bypass all the major centres of traffic like New York, Boston, Washington, Baltimore and Richmond. By the time we reached North Carolina, our road trip seemed less than a great idea but we continued on enjoying the trip anyway. We enjoyed the scenery but Nancy was growing tired of the driving. After all, she drove the full distance herself. I was not healthy enough to do the long-distance driving, especially driving in what was, at times, very heavy traffic. We programed our evening stops into the Garmin (GPS) each morning and that worked out well for us each day except Saturday. We got into the Washington area and our Garmin took us the wrong route. I guess we should have looked at the map more closely prior to the start of each day's driving. We did have a Triptik from CAA that I reviewed daily, but it was hard for me to follow with my cognitive issues.

The first overnight stop was in Bangor, Maine, USA. I was so tired and my legs were stiff. We checked in and then found a place to have dinner. Back at the hotel laying down, I was questioning my decision to take this road trip. Maybe it was a little too much for me yet. Maybe I should go back home because I was not feeling all that great. I woke twice during the night but overall had a good sleep. On waking, I decided not to say anything to Nancy about my thoughts and how I felt the night before. I did not want to ruin her trip. We had breakfast and pushed ahead, driving 10 hours to Scranton, PA on Friday. It seems the first day of travel was the worst and I did not get as tired during rest of the trip, but my legs were stiff and aching each day. When we stopped to rest each night, I used Voltaren Emulgel on my legs and it helped. We noticed how the vegetation was changing to more greenery as we drove further south, which was a welcome sight indeed considering it was minus 12 Celsius in Halifax the morning we left home.. This change improved our morale and made us feel happy.

On Sunday morning, not long passed the state line of South Carolina, we noticed many signs advertising Duke's BBQ. It was about lunch time so we were convinced to drop by and check it out. We programed our Garmin to find the place. Driving into the parking area at Duke's BBQ, we noted it was not very busy. Just after arriving the place begin to fill up. Church goers, we learned, had just finished their morning church service. We weren't sure how this place worked as to getting our food, and a few southerners noticed this and were very willing to help us out. It was help yourself buffet for $12.50 — all you can eat. Americans like buffets, we learned. We were not familiar with some of the food, but people in line were happy to assist us in explaining the food. There were hush puppies, collard greens and fried okra, and the best fried chicken we'd ever eaten. Duke's was our first sample of real South Carolina food and hospitality. We loved the people; they were friendly, smiling and gracious. Nancy and I dug into our heaping plates of food. It was so delicious. It was the best meal we had on our road trip. Nancy noted this may make us sleepy for the remainder of our drive, but none-the-less we continued eating the great food. After our meal, as we left to continue on our way, some folks wished us well. We were contented, with a full belly and happy we had decided to stop at Duke's BBQ. It became one of the highlights of our trip because of the food, southern friendliness and the hospitality of the local folks. We planned to visit again on our trip home but it was mid-morning when we passed by the turn off and it was too early to get BBQ we thought. We told other tourists about Duke's on our trip, and also to our friends since we got home.

Arriving at Hilton Head, it was 85°F with clear blue skies. It was great to feel the warm sun considering our long winter. It was really good to be in a warm, sunny place. We checked into out rental, a condo just a few minutes' walk from the beach that had a backyard pool. We soon were lying next to the pool in the heat of the mid-afternoon sun. Awesome indeed!! We needed this. Next was to find groceries, then the beach. A short walk to the beach revealed the most beautiful beach of white sand that stretched for miles. We would spend lots of time here over the next three weeks lying in the sun, swimming or in the warm ocean water, and riding our rented bikes on the hard-packed sand during low tide. Hilton Head is a biking mecca with many biking trails, and many folks rode on the beach at low tide. The biking proved too difficult for me but I did it anyway. We had brought bike helmets with us from Canada, where helmets are mandatory for all citizens. After all I did have a brain injury so it was a good ideal for me to wear a helmet. Most Americans and tourists in Hilton Head do no wear helmets. Nancy really wanted to bike. I was trying just for her. Bike riding made my legs ache but we thought the exercise would be good for me in the long term. It is difficult and disheartening to always have aches in the legs. If one does not have them they do not and will not understand. Many times while bike riding, I lost my balance. It was a lack of balance that came out of nowhere for no reason at all. We soon understood that this was as a result of my brain injury. When I felt my balance go I could not correct it. This resulted in a wipeout face first into the hard-packed beach sand. This one time I wiped out while crossing the street and it was a hard fall onto the pavement. I got back up and on the bike and continued home. I had no injury except for a skinned leg. After the fall on the pavement, I was a little nervous of riding on paved areas, so we walked our bike to the nearby beach. I have to say that bicycling on the beach, riding along the ocean, was very enjoyable even when I knew the leg aches would follow.

> **A quote from Nelson Mandela:**
>
> *"Do not judge me by my successes, judge me by how many times I fell down and got back up again."*

Falling down and getting back up happened many times a day during my trip to Hilton Head Island. Nancy always tried to stay positive about it for me. She enjoyed the biking for sure. After bike riding we would lay on the beach, lay next to the pool or soak in the pool to cool down and relax. I noticed she was a great swimmer. I had not been in water since the stroke, so I soon realized my swimming abilities had diminished when I tried. I could not coordinate my body enough.

All the activity and noting my decreased abilities made me tired, and resulted in increased frustration levels and increased irritability. It was really bothering me some days, but I tried to stay positive. When I became tired and frustrated I would get cranky. This frustration is, unfortunately, taken out on the person closest to you. I like the following bible verses: Proverbs 12:18: "Restless words pierce like a sword but the tongue of the wise brings healing." Also: James 1:19: "My brothers, take note of this: everyone should be quick to listen, slow to speak and slow to anger." Those are words to live by, but very difficult for a brain injury survivor. It requires much focused concentration to realize it is time to step back, say I need a time out because I am feeling very frustrated and cranky, but it is the best thing to do. Please do the best you can, even if you do not have an ABI. One morning I criticised her for trying to feed a turtle. She loves animals and apparently did not see or read the sign "DO NOT FEED THE ANIMALS." Anyway, she did not handle it well (to say the least.) Even after returning to Nova Scotia for some time after she kept reminding me of that morning.

I have to say that, overall, I enjoyed the trip; it had lots of positives for us both.

The trip to Hilton Head did not go as well as we thought. Maybe our expectations were too high considering my health issues that past year. I did make it there and back that in itself is a win for me and for us. I did have some concerns at the beginning, but my thinking was, I can only find out what I can do by trying. "Let's do this" I said with as much enthusiasm as I could muster.

As a result of the stroke in my right front brain hemisphere and taking Citalopram (Celaxa), I did not have a lot of empathy most of the time. You may notice this sometimes in my writing. In discussion with my GP and on his advice, I stopped taking the drug after our return from vacation. Nancy and I have noticed that my empathy and a little more of the real me is returning. I like that. It feels good to know the real me is in there somewhere. My brain is finding new paths to let it work properly. Another Hurrah.

Since returning home I found a product named VitaPulse that I thought would be good for me after reading about it, but it just turned out to be snake oil. It is sold as a cure-all but was just another crap product sold to rip consumers of. I threw it all out in the trash.

My leg aches subsided somewhat and in summer 2016. I began to play some golf again, going alone to golf courses and hooking up with some retired folks. I occasionally joined up with my son. Playing only nine holes each outing when my energy levels are ok to do it was the best I could do. The golf also helps my legs and boosts my confidence. I can walk nine holes ok most of the time, with a bag cart caddy towing behind me. I will need a power cart when I graduate to eighteen holes, but I am playing. Any day I can play golf is a good day, indeed a milestone, a Hurrah Moment. I like that and so does Stefan. I love him so much. He is the best son any man could ever want or have.

I also noticed I have low energy, low motivation issues and low libido. I have to investigate to find a solution to that. I did mention this to my GP on one visit but he seemed not to be as concerned as I was, nor take it seriously. I have learned lack of motivation is a common trait of brain injury survivors. Nancy and I did some research and found a Doctor Christian Hackshaw, at Advanced MD, whose practice deals mostly with anti-aging. He is a holistic doctor and also a licensed GP who once worked in a big hospital emergency room setting. He said Western doctors are taught to treat symptoms not find causes. They prescribe pills for the symptoms then more pills for the side effects of the first pills given. On my visit he noted most of the issues I described seemed to be a hormonal imbalance. He also noted that at the time I had the stroke was a time in a man's life when hormones are changing and imbalanced. This may be causing, low energy, lack of motivation, low libido, loss of muscle, and muscle aches (like pain in legs etc.). He has had lot of experience with that issue and will try to find answers for me. He gave me a test kit to get my hormone levels checked. It's a good idea, I thought, and I could hardly wait to see the testing results. If hormones are out of balance, let's get them set right again. Any help at this point was appreciated. At this point I need answers that normal Western doctors do not have. On a recent visit to my family GP, I informed him of my visit to Dr. Hackshaw. My GP agreed that I may have a hormone imbalance. Why did he not listen to me and look into it, I thought. Maybe he needed another opinion. My GP now really would like to see the report, he said. My family GP has been a good doctor and I have confidence in him. The results of the hormone test showed I do have a hormone imbalance and I was placed on a three-month program of medication to improve that imbalance. Note: since taking the meds he gave me, I found some of it proved to not be beneficial. With his advice I stopped taking the adrenal support pills. I also discussed the test results and the medicine I was prescribed with my GP, who had words of caution. I did not finish the program, it seems it stimulated my brain too much. I had to lay down later in the day most days because my head felt funny and my brain was too stimulated. I'll have to find another cure, I thought, because the public system will not. I will have to find my own solutions.

In May 2017, we decided to take another road trip to Hilton Head, South Carolina. On day three we stopped in West Virginia at a Wendy's for lunch. As I got out of the car, I noticed a gentleman sitting on a stone wall at the edge of the property near the restaurant. He was wearing a military fatigue jacket, he had a beard and seemed to look older than his years. After lunch, we were returning to our car and I noticed he was kind of staring out and looked sad, so I went over to speak to him asking how he was doing. The man stated that he just got in last night.

"From where?" I asked.

"Nashville Tennessee," he said. "I was there for eight and a half years and I hitchhiked back here. My wife died down there."

"Sorry to hear," I stated.

"I have her ashes in my pack sack," he said, removing and showing me her urn. I noticed the sack was falling apart. "I will have to go to the local Salvation Army down the road, maybe they have a better one," he said. "Her daughter lives around here, I am not sure where, but I promised my wife I would bring her ashes home and find her daughter to let her know her mother died. I am not sure where she lives but my wife told me of a guy who works at a muffler shop here that knows her. I will find her."

I asked him if he had any food (knowing he did not, or none that I could see)

"I am not asking or begging for anything," he said.

"Yes, I know, but I want to get you lunch," I said. I took $15 US out of my pocket and handed it to him.

"I would like to get one of those Baconator burgers," he said, pointing to the Wendy's sign.

I gave the money to him and told him to get something to eat. I asked him if he was from here also, and he said no.

"My mom lives in Maryland, a good woman she is. We have not visited or talked to each other for some time. I will go there to visit when I get done here," he said. "My mother went to Canada a few times when I was a kid," he said.

He thanked me as he walked away. I was getting into the car and he turned and said "God bless you, Jesus loves you," as he disappeared into Wendy's to get some lunch. Since that Saturday morning I have thought of this conversation and that man many times. Here was a man down on his luck, his wife's ashes in an urn in his backpack, he had nothing but his belief in God and Jesus so he had everything. I ask myself if I could keep faith and belief under those circumstances, or would I be totally angry at God and Jesus for letting me get into those circumstances. How would you feel? I have thought of this man often since and wondered if he did ok or if I could have done more.

> **A common saying I heard in my youth was a quote by Helen Keller:**
>
> *"I cried because I had no shoes until I saw a man with no feet."*

I also remembered my grandmother words: help strangers when you can if they need a helping hand. You never know when they are in the presence of an angel, because angels walk this earth. Helping someone in need is God-like. We often ask if there is an afterlife. What happens to us once we are dead? That question scares most of us, but not. Some, as I have, find peace with a belief in Jesus and God, but then I had a near-death experience that changed my perspective on life, death and the afterlife. A friend of mine had her father in palliative care. After hearing him praying, a gentleman in a bed next to him asked: "How do you get to heaven? He answered "me, I believe in God and Jesus. As for the transportation of it, I leave that to him." Great wit even on his death bed. Imagine this man's belief and resolve. What would any of the rest of us say in that moment?

# CHAPTER THIRTY-ONE

It has now been more than two years since the stroke. Recovery is not easy, there is no quick fix. It has been a difficult time. I still have days of tiredness and fatigue, not so much brain fog anymore. My crankiness brought on by the stroke has subsided greatly in no small part due to my work to control it. I still get really frustrated and difficult when I am tired, and I take time outs. I still have leg stiffness and joint pain, but I pray about it and work on positive self-talk about it often. The constant leg issues really bother me, and I look forward to it dissipating and being gone all together. I believe I will get there. Recently, I became aware of a new device that was said to really help chronic pain sufferers. It is named QUELL. A Google search will reveal information about it. This device has really helped. It's the first time in two years that my legs are almost pain-free on some occasions. Without feeling the constant chronic pain, I feel kind of weird sometimes. The thing is, I have noticed I had learned to live with my leg pain, but I sure can live without it. In the fall of 2016, I started to have neck issues that continued a few days a week all winter and spring. It was very painful. I visited my GP many times about it but, as usual, there are not many solutions in the Public health care system. Again, I would have to find a solution myself. I visited physiotherapy doctors many times and a chiropractor many times, but all this began to get expensive for a fellow without income. The public health system was a failure once again, so I had to try to fix things myself. I found a tens unit that helped and then in July 2017 I started acupuncture at the Quality Life Healing Centre with Dr. Feng Jia. He uses the ancient way of acupuncture. This technique has left my neck pain free for a few weeks now, another hurray but no thanks to Public health system. My family and I have found a way to pay for the necessary treatment ourselves with $20 covered per visit by my Blue Cross, not a lot but a help. Acupuncture usually costs from $75 - $90 dollars per visit, so at two visits a week costs can add up. The Public health system is a complete failure for ABI folks, especially after release from hospital. We have to find and pay for our own solutions.

Since being home and recovering, I have found some things on my own that are helpful. These may help you if you are recovering from a stroke or other ABI. It is not a complete list. I am sure other folks have found other things that help them cope with their ABI. Use my suggestions at your own risk, these are just some things I have found, but they may or may not work for you. As usual, consult with your doctor before attempting the items that I have listed that worked for me. I found myself with no Public health system help, and if it helped I kept doing it until I reached a plateau when it seemed to be of no benefit. Then I found a new solution that worked, trial and error so to speak, but it is necessary when one is in constant pain and has health issues without a real solution. The Public system seems to be about keeping patients returning as often and for as long term as possible, and making pharmaceutical companies rich.

1. Exercise at the gym, not over doing it. Do the best you can. I walked five laps around the track, then 10 to 15 minutes on a stationary bike. After that I would exercise with some light weights, then a few stretches, after which I usually got into the hot tub for 10 minutes. The hot tub helped relax my muscles. Exercise is really good for our neurology. Check with your doctor before attempting exercise. Consult your doctor and they will advise what exercise is best for you, if any.

2. A vegan protein shake about two to three times a week. The one I use I get at Walmart

3. Writing this book has been helpful for me, At least write down your feelings and what is going on with you. That will help.

4. The QUELL that I strap to my leg has really helped with the chronic leg, muscle and joint pain.

5. Staying active, doing things for myself.

6. Social group like BIANS and church groups.

7. Attending BIANS group information sessions. Also, there is a group named "Head On" that meets the second and fourth Wednesday of each month. This group is more of a social group, a good opportunity to talk with other survivors.

8. Going to a warm climate for vacations, sitting in the sun with a good sunscreen applied.
    This may be difficult for many brain injury victims due to lack of money.

9. Preparing dinner for myself and occasionally family members.

10. Talking to other folks that have lived with brain injury for a long time. Learn about their struggles and Hurrah Moments.

11. Setting up a schedule for my daily activities and sticking to it.

12. Being as independent as possible.

13. Getting the ok to drive again was freeing.

14. Schedule a rest daily, follow that even when I did not want to.

15. Scheduled two short walks daily with the dog.

16. To bed early. That was 10 P.M. for me or before depending how I was feeling

17. Limit TV watching, no news programs especially no US news media. Sometimes TV was all I had, especially on bad weather days.

18. Keeping and going to doctor appointments, as required.

19. Taking my prescription meds on time, working with my doctors and figuring out which meds I did need and not need to take as time passed.

20. Working with Nova Scotia Rehab Centre ABI outreach group. These folks were available for a couple of months usually once or twice a week, then nothing.

21. Staying as active as possible.

22. Working hard to control my frustrations and crankiness. When I felt cranky I usually took a time out. I also let my family member know how I was feeling and that I needed a time out. When alone I would go to lay down or sit in a comfortable chair in a quiet room and meditate about it.

23. Personal positive reinforcement.

24. Reading many books and keeping brain active.

25. Mindfulness meditation.

26. Praying a lot, and having faith. It will be difficult sometimes but stay focused on it.

27. Attending church.

28. Taking part in church groups where I was not judged but helped and listened to. This was also good for improving social group skills.

29. Doing what I can around the house or at least attempting to do the things I could do prior to the stroke and brain surgery.

30. Not complaining or at least minimize my complaining as much as possible. In most cases, but not always, there is somebody worse off than you. Like rereading

and thinking about the quote by Helen Keller "I cried because I had no shoes until I saw a man with no feet". This was to keep me focused on the positive in my life

31. Hug family members and others as much as possible. Giving back as much as possible for their love and support is important.

    One would be surprised how much this helps

32. Do not be too needy.

33. Say thank you and give compliments as often as possible and as necessary.

34. A very important one: do the best you can.

35. Believe in yourself.

> **A quote from Nelson Mandela:**
>
> *"Do not be resentful. Resentment is like drinking poison and then hoping it will kill your enemy."*

> **Quote from Nelson Mandela:**
>
> *"Do not judge me by my successes, judge me by how many times I fell down and got back up again."*

36. At the end of each day, have the courage to say, "I will try again tomorrow."

37. I would remove myself to a bedroom to lay down, or to a comfortable chair in another room for a little space as needed. It is better to do that then yell at those closest to you. They will like you better for it and you will like yourself better also.

38. Although I thought I was alone, I soon realised I was not. That in itself is of great help. Check out your local brain injury association for social groups and reach out for help. Just being with others that understand what you are going through is good for the soul, and is also a help for care givers and your family members. I prayed and asked Jesus to take the wheel for my difficult road ahead. A peace came over me at that time, and I just knew I would be OK.

39. Ear plugs. In crowds like in a restaurant, shop or other crowded areas, the noise really bothered me; it caused fatigue and frustration. Nancy went to a music store and bought me a set of drummer ear plugs. Those drowned out the white noise but I could hear and talk to people sitting close to me. These worked great.

40. The symptoms that will hold anybody back from recovery the most are: fear, anger, hatred, sadness, jealously, conflict and separation from other people. We should enjoy the moment we are in, it is all we have. The past is gone and the future is not here yet. I remember the following (not sure where it came from): "The past is gone but we have this moment. This moment is a gift, which is why we call it the present." The best I have ever received is the gift of life. It is good to plan a little for the future but is not helpful to us to live in the past or future. You do not have any of this in any moment you are in.

> **I really like the following quote from Wendy Renzulla:**
>
> *"Brain injury survivors are the most extraordinary people surviving under the most terrible circumstances and they become more extraordinary because of it."*

Food for thought indeed.

41. Recently I started having some hip and lower back pain. I woke up one day and it was stiff and painful. I made an appointment with a chiropractor at Sound Chiropractic to check it out. Dr. Ellen gave me a good check over and assessment, and she noted that my left leg was shorter than my right leg. This may be causing the problems I am having. She said it is common for stroke victims to have a shorter leg on the side most affected by the stroke. At the beginning, we talked about the fact I did not want any neck manipulation of any kind, but it was not necessary she told me. She set to work. Checking my posture, my leg lengths, my knees, my full back (including my lower back and hips. After just a few appointments I am feeling much better. I wish I had known about this earlier. Shortly after the stroke I was checked out by an Occupational Therapist, a Physiotherapist, Massage Therapy, hospital doctors and my GP many times at the QEII and in rehab but none noticed that problem. I wish I had that diagnoses earlier in my recovery process. That knowledge probably would have helped a lot to get it corrected much earlier and probably shortened my recovery process.

Why the Public system of health care professionals had not noticed this at the beginning I do not know. I did visit a chiropractor in late 2016 and early in 2017 but she did not notice my leg issue or at least did not mention it at the time. Dr Ellen is getting me back on track now so that is excellent.

42. One of the biggest problems I've had since the brain injury was not a health-related but was with the Desjardins Insurance Company. I purchased the right insurance policy some years ago. I just chose the wrong insurance company to purchase it from. I was content that I would not have to worry if anything happened to my health. I informed my children about it a number of times and kept a policy copy in my safety deposit box. My daughter has a key. After the brain injury, I submitted a claim but Desjardins denied my claim and again denied my claim on appeal. I filed legal action and did get something but not a lot. I hope this information will help you make the right decision for you and your family on insurance.

On a more positive note I also had insurance from Blue Cross: medical, dental, hospital, travel, extended health, and critical care. Blue Cross have been excellent to date, thank God. They are very professional and very helpful in my recovery. Their staff have always processed my claims in a timely manner, answered my calls, and advised me of any claims I was entitled to make. I would recommend Blue Cross to anybody.

I want to inform as many people as possible as to the necessity of having a good insurance policy with a good company. People may need to review their current policies and company. Avoid some and learn from what has happened to me. Google a company to check how many legal actions they have against them and any positive or negative recommendations by customers. Check for any reviews available before you make any decisions on health insurance. To date, I have spent some $20,000 on medical professionals I needed that was not covered by the Public system, and sometimes the people in the Public system are not very good; I needed better advice and better care

# CHAPTER THIRTY-TWO

Many of my best years have passed. I am now 61 and I understand how wise my grandparents were. I often say, "Where has the time gone?" This is especially so when I see my grown kids at 35 and 38, and my four-year-old granddaughter.

It seems my kids were children just yesterday, when I tucked them in bed, read a good night story, taught them their bedtime prayers, then just before turning out the light for the night I gave them a kiss and received goodnight Butterfly kisses.

Later in the evening as I was going to bed we would look in on the kids. They always looked so contented and peacefully sleeping, so innocent. It just fills your heart up with love for them. It brings a tear to my eye now just remembering those times. We would check to ensure the bed covers were pulled around them, give them a little peck on the check. I would whisper under my breath to my son, "Goodnight my son," and to my daughter, "Goodnight daddy's little princess." I miss those nights, if only I could have one of those back. Now I say this in prayer each night "God bless my children, Stefan and Suzanne, and also my granddaughter, Charlotte. Goodnight my little princess Charlotte, God bless you." I say this every night when I go to bed at my own house alone, or anywhere I am. Those are a few of my last words for the day.

Sometimes my daughter complains about Charlotte and it brings a smile to my face because it brings me memories of when she was a little girl. I thought things like that were important but really were not, so I relate this story (I think I read it in a Reader's Digest monthly version many years ago but still remember it). A 30-something man, married with young children, complained about his kids playing on the lawn; they were ruining the grass. But now as an old man he looks out his window and wishes his children were young again and back playing on the lawn again, just one more time. Oh, how he would change that complaining because it seemed so irrelevant and unimportant now. The lawn is green now and the grass is so lovely, and would be even if the kids had grown up playing there.

The thing about time is that when it is gone, it is gone. Nobody can rewind it, no matter how hard you may wish for or want the time back. The moments are fleeting indeed. The best you can do is have great memories, and that is up to you how those are made. One can sit and think about the past, dwell on what you think were mistakes for hours or days, but you cannot change nor will anything about your past change. Do not pack everything in a bag as it happens and then drag it around with you. The best is to forgive yourself for the perceived mistakes made and accept the life you have. You probably did the best you could at the time. Be contented with life and all you have, have some gratitude. Be grateful although life may not be what you hoped for. It is the best for you. Each day is a new life, a new chance. It is up to you to live each day with gratitude and always do the best you can.

It is good to feel some happiness again, even if only occasionally. As for happiness, I know it is not filled by an external source but peace with our God, internal peace and tranquility. I call this contentment. I have seen many people, including me, plan trips and be so excited about going only to return to the same grind. Within a few weeks, voices of discontentment are heard again. The richest folks are the unhappiest. Some of the happiest folks I have met are those that do not have millions but those that are happy with their partner. They love and enjoy their family and make time for God; these are the happiest folks I have met. That, my friends, is a simple recipe anybody can follow.

Now I do believe people want to feel a purpose and that does help them be happy. The best thing for that is service to others, such as at a church, a charity, or some other volunteer work.

Spend time with family, find joy in them. Give to others according to your means. You will feel better and will be rewarded for it, if not in this life, then the next.

Remember the Bible verse Luke: 21, verses 1-4: "As Jesus looked up, he saw the rich putting their gifts into the temple treasury. 2 He also saw a poor widow put in two very small copper coins. 3 "Truly I tell you," he said, "this poor widow has put in more than all the others. 4 All these people gave their gifts out of their wealth; but she out of her poverty put in all she had to live on."

# CHAPTER THIRTY-THREE

My granddaughter, Charlotte, was born in August 2013. My little girl had her own little girl, a real beauty! We had a princess Charlotte long time before there was a Royal Princess Charlotte. Holding Charlotte as an infant was such a rewarding experience. It reminded me of my own daughter — my own princess — at that age. She has been a real joy to my life. She is four now and likes to tell everybody "I am four." It is strange when we are little that we cannot wait to be older but when we get older we wish we had our younger years back. My heart melts every time I see Charlotte. It has been said that if I knew grandchildren were so much fun I would have had them first. The moment I saw her I was in love with this child and have been since. Whenever I see her she dances and yells "Papa, Papa." I love those words. That makes a papa so happy. Just a while back, Nancy and Suzanne and I took Charlotte to a movie called "Norm of the North." It was her first movie at a theatre. Wow!

Is all I can say, what a wonderful experience! The amazement of a child's is truly something to see and experience.

On Christmas Eve 2016, Charlotte said, "Papa, tomorrow we need a cake because it is baby Jesus' birthday." I asked her who told her that, and she said the man in church that wears the long dress. Apparently, my ex-wife, her grandma, was taking her to Mass fairly often and especially during the previous six months while Suzanne was away on military course. I guess she was listening to the priest after all. On Christmas, we were all invited to Suzanne's for dinner, so I made and brought a birthday cake for baby Jesus' birthday. It read Happy Birthday Jesus. Charlotte said, "Papa, I will have to blow out the candles because baby Jesus is too little." I placed some candles on the cake and as she blew them out we sang happy birthday to Jesus. Suzanne took a short video and apparently posted it on Facebook. It is great that Charlotte is learning that Christmas is not just about presents but has a deeper meaning, a meaning a lot of folks do not celebrate or take part in. Our society is so concerned about Political Correctness. Christmas is a Christian holiday and a celebration for all Christians who should please forget political correctness and celebrate it. Tell your children what Christmas really is about, attend a church service, be proud of your Christian roots, and please wear it as a badge of honour as I do. Christians do not tell other religions how to celebrate their holy days so why do Christians worry about what other religions think about ours, or how we celebrate? It is our right to celebrate as we want to, in our own Christian way.

# CHAPTER THIRTY-FOUR

od knows what your prayers mean. He listens to your needs and understands you, what you are expecting from him what your needs are. Prayer should not be an asking session all the time, but time for reaffirmation of your intentions. Instead of asking for something, just say, "God what can I do to help this world be a better place?" I remember to always only think positive thoughts as I fall off to sleep. I believe the last few minutes of the day just prior to falling asleep are the most important minutes of the day also to give some gratitude for the day's events.

In January 2016, I joined a men's prayer group at Saint Benedict's Church. We meet every Friday morning at 7 A.M. It's early I know, and it has been difficult for me to get there sometimes but I go as often as I can. Occasionally I have doctor appointments that morning so I need to rest a little longer. Other times I just do not want to get out of bed, due to feeling tired or fatigued. Sometimes I just do not want to go. That's OK.

Socializing is good for me. It helps my mood and cognition. Besides, prayer is always good for a person and helpful. Faith in a higher power is not a bad thing. I feel like I have been to hell and back and still breathing.

# CHAPTER THIRTY-FIVE

A single mom, Stella, and a little girl, Hannah, who are from Africa, a black family, moved in next door to me. I could not write a story without mentioning this child. She was about six years old when they moved in next store. I soon got to chat with Hannah and her mom and got to know them. At Christmas, I decided to get a present for Hannah, a set of head phones, and I gave them to her.

"How did you know I wanted those?" she said.

She was so happy. Apparently she had not received a Christmas gift before in her life, she was so happy. The next day Stella told me Hannah wanted to go the lobby of our building to get her photo taken with her present next to the Christmas tree. She posed many times for photos. After that Hannah and I were great friends. Her face always lights up with a beautiful smile when she sees me and we always giving each other a hug. I see her often as she arrives home from school with her mom, and I always enquire about how school is going. This child is a joy indeed. I have given Hannah a gift for all Christmas' since and some money at the end of school year for her success. Last Christmas I also gave a gift to Stella, who was very surprised by that. She gave a big smile and a Thank-you hug. That is what makes Christmas: making people smile and happy. Giving is always more rewarding than receiving. On my first weekend home from the hospital with my kids and Nancy, I insisted on going to my own place. There was a handmade card slipped under my door from Hannah. The card read "Get Well Soon" and included a drawing of a heart and a two stick people: one pink stick person and one blue stick person holding hands under a smiling sun. She wrote, "I hope you feel much better. Signed your friend Hannah." It made me shed a tear indeed. Hannah was so happy to see me, and there was that big smile and hug. I was much better already after that. Stella told me Hannah was worried about me, not knowing what had happened and insisted on praying for me every night. Aww, I thought, God had to answer her prayers. How could he not answer the prayers of such a sweet, innocent child? It was another big reason why I was recovering.

Although I am home to my own place since late last year, I see Hannah often now. She always has a smile and I get a hug. Sometimes Hannah and Stella come over for me to help with her school work. I have learned since the stroke and by helping Hannah that I have an issue performing math skills now, but I enjoy those moments with Hannah. Stella does not have much education it seems, probably because of her growing up in Africa. It was difficult to realize I cannot even perform Grade five 5 math. I had always been good at math skills during my grade school and college years. I got one score of 100% for a college physics course and did well in other math-based college courses such as Calculus, Electro-tech and Strengths of Materials.

Hannah is a beautiful child that really likes to have her hair braided by her mom, who does such a great job of it. Hannah really is a very smart and intelligent kid. She finished Grade 4 this year, June 2017, and is going into Grade 5 this year fall of 2017. A few days ago, she came over to show me her end of year grades. They were really good and she, deservedly, was very proud of herself as was I. It was due to her great work this year. I gave her a hug and a little congratulations money for her great work. She has a chance that many girls in Africa do not. I am sure she will do something that will change the world in a good way. I wish I had the money to place in an education fund for the university education she will need later. She has already changed my world. I believe every time a person makes a child smile you gain favour with God and it helps change the world. Boosting a person up is always a good thing to do.

# CHAPTER THIRTY-SIX

During the summer of 2015, Nancy's daughter, Catlin, was in Africa working at a refugee camp under UN control. It was a camp of 25,000 refugee persons. She was working on a research paper for her master's degree. During the summer, she introduced us to Akika, a young Rwandan refugee who had a baby boy, Ben. Her story is a book and I will not write much about her life struggle without her input and approval because I probably would get some things wrong. Over the summer we exchanged photos and I sent money to help ease the struggle that this family was going through. The money was sent through Catlin. That was the best because Akika received all the money to do with as was her requirements for her and little Ben. She was attending school in the camp, so needed a grad dress, food and other requirements — only basic needs really. Sending money this way was great; there was no agency taking a big portion of the funds. I noted little Ben's only toy was a pill box with pebbles inside and taped closed. I wanted to ensure Catlin brought some toys for him and she did. That made me feel so proud of Catlin and we were happy to help this family as much as we could. Akika is now in Canada attending University in British Columbia. We invited her and Ben to come to Halifax for Christmas of 2015. We wanted her and Ben have a great first Christmas in Canada, and they sure did. They received many presents and saw snow for the first time. Ben went playing in the snow with his new family, laughing, falling down, and making snow balls and angels. Awesome! Ben and Akika also received the gift of a family for Christmas, and many hugs over the Christmas season. We were sad to see them go back to British Columbia. She has now finished her first year of University with great marks and was just recently accepted to the faculty for a chance at her nursing degree. She will succeed I am sure and I pray for her success. Akika has a boyfriend now, a fellow that apparently came from the same refugee camp she was in. He was living and going to school in another Canadian province but they found each other on Facebook, I am told. Amazing indeed! She and Ben are now doing very well. Catlin stays in contact with her and keeps us informed of the progress. Nancy also follows her on Facebook.

After the snowfall and a night's sleep, the next morning Akika came down stairs. She looked outside, noted the snow and said, "It's still here!" With that we all laughed, and Nancy said it will be here until about April. This seemed to really startle Akika.

"Really!" she said.

As Christmas ended, Akika and Ben sadly were soon heading to Vancouver Island where Akika was to start University soon.

# CHAPTER THIRTY-SEVEN

During the years I was working I had always invested a portion of my money into RRSPs and a savings account. This money has helped sustained me over the past 2+ years, along with some small sums from CPP and family help. My meds costs are supplemented by my Blue Cross insurance. It has been a God send not to have to worry too much about income when something out of the ordinary happened with my health. I am not rich by any means, but wish I was because than I would have to worry less about the future. I remember while in hospital hearing many conversations between husbands and wives or partners about lack of money. Sometimes I could hear crying about the stress, not having money to pay the bills, mortgages and such. Many men in the hospital I knew were the only bread-winner for the family. It's a lot of stress to have that on your plate during a brain injury recovery. To have to worry about rent or maybe a mortgage, Internet, cable, power, heat, maybe property taxes, water bill etc., . It may force a person to want to try to go back to work long before they are able or ready. I have not been able to return to work yet. I am not sure what the future holds for me, but I think about it often with some anxiety. I decided to leave it in God's hands and I know all will be well. It will work out. He has a greater plan for me and it is why I survived the stroke and brain surgery. At one point, I applied to Canada Pension for a disability pension. A social worker at the rehab centre helped me complete the paperwork and the claim was subsequently approved for a monthly sum. This has been a great help. It almost covers my rent. I have an apartment where I've lived since 2011. I needed to and have kept paying since my brain injury, although I soon may have to look for cheaper accommodations. My own place that I can afford is important to my peace of mind and my confidence. Knowing I have a place to live independently. I also need money for healthcare like physio, dental, massages, acupuncture and such. My health plan only covers a percentage of the cost. Of the many medical needs I have, not all the cost is covered by the Public health care system or my insurance, and this has been a strain on the funds I had saved. This is another area the Canadian Public system falls well short.

# CHAPTER THIRTY-EIGHT

For a week in the winter of 2016--17, Nancy and I parted. It was a sad day indeed. We have worked things through as I struggle to find and access all the help I need. Nancy had a problem accepting the new me, so do I. I think she tried very hard to understand the new me, and did the best she could, but she may not be equipped for the realities of our new life, my new life. I have less compassion, more frustration, I am more critical and more negative, and sometimes I'm angry about my life changes. These are traits that have been left to me as a result of the brain surgery and the stroke. I have been working hard and really trying. I hope I can and will get back to normal or at least that which was normal for me. It has been a struggle, lots of hard work and soul-searching, indeed, as nobody will or can really understand. They are not me, have not felt the struggle, the pain, the frustration, the anger and the disappointment when your life's carpet is pulled out from under your feet. She would like the old me back and I am not sure that is possible. Is the old me in there somewhere, or am I gone forever? I have some work to do and have really tried through these most difficult times. Nancy has a small business of three employees plus herself that keeps her employed. She also has an aged mother that relies on her, there is nobody else. She tries hard and works very hard.

This past week, Nancy and I talked. She explained her feelings and thoughts that I may need to see a psychologist to help me work out some issues. I agreed and will seek help to work out the issues. We went, but other than the $170 an hour for the doctor, not much was gained from it.

We have now made up, moved on and are happy to be together. So far, so good.

I'm mourning the loss of my previous life. It is difficult to accept indeed. Having a brain injury is life-changing. Statistics show I probably will never have a full recovery from the brain injury and it's a scary thought. Then again, what is normal really? I have a new normal now. I really do love this woman.

Over the past two years I have learned that family is the most important asset a person has. I have always known this but now it has been reinforced very strongly. My kids and Nancy have been a rock for me. Helping me get through what I have and recover the way I have is a result of their support and love. People whom have no kids and want no kids will regret that decision when they get old or if they become ill during their lives. All humans will get old someday if we live a long life, it is a given for sure. It is important to have a family who cares when one is seriously ill or old. Getting old is good because that means I am still alive, hurray I made it.

It is important to have a good relationship with our kids, even if they are assholes sometimes. I can assure all, our kids will be assholes sometimes. Get through those times as best you can without unnecessary bitter feelings that some may carry for years. Learn to let things go, build good relationships and bridges. There's no need to pack bags to carry around with you, they weigh you down. Besides, extra bags are costly when boarding a plane.

# CHAPTER THIRTY-NINE

## *My Gratitude*

I have learned life can change in random order in a second, as my life did. Your life can too, no matter who you are or what you have. It really is not random to God. He has a plan and we just do not know the details. I tell people that eventually it will be their turn, it will not always be somebody other than you. The person whom something happens to also thought it was always going to be somebody else. I did too, but it wasn't somebody other than me, it was me. It makes one come to terms with and realize their own mortality.

Although each day is somewhat of a struggle but improving, I have learned to enjoy each moment of each day as must as possible. The moments will become minutes, then hours, then days, to weeks to months to years etc. You get the picture. I am happy and thankful I have more days on the earth to share with the people I love. A life-changing health event sure changed my perspective on life itself. Nobody will ever see a U-Haul travelling behind a hearse carrying the stuff you once owned. Nothing can be taken with us into the spirit world, we shed all our worldly belongings. When you arrive, you will not have any status, money or stuff. You will finally shed your ego and all other human needs and wants. Your status, money and stuff is all left behind to the human world, it is of no value in the afterlife. Why do you think people, like Warren Buffett and others with a lot of money, start to give it away as they get old? They know it is going to be of no value to them soon. I do not have to think about that because I am not a man that has an abundance of stuff or money, but I do have what is important: a great, loving family, and an abundance of love and kindness for my family and humanity.

Try to stay positive, even when it is difficult to do so. Negativity just brings you and everybody around you down. Sometimes I may be a little negative, but I ensure those times are minimized. Even when negative I try to joke about it after somebody points out I am a little pessimistic sometimes. I usually will answer, "No, I am not a pessimist just an experienced optimist. It is ok to be an experienced optimist, it keeps me in reality."

Hug your children, tell them and show them you love them often, even if they are grown men and women. I have always done or tried to do that. Maybe it is why they have been there for me these past few years since my ABI and continue to be. I love them and appreciate them so much.

I am grateful for my children, for their love, their strength and the courage they have shown and given me.

I am grateful for Nancy coming into my life, for her love, compassion, courage and reinforcing to me the need for positive thinking, even when it was not easy for her. She has been a rock of support for me and has helped push me forward in my recovery even as she was running her own business. She really is one of the prime reasons I have recovered such as I have, through the stroke and subsequent brain surgery. She makes me feel like I am home. Thank you.

I have learned that trying to write a book is difficult. I have limited typing skills (and no formal training) and I'm not highly skilled in computer systems or use. With limited writing skills, plus having a brain injury, writing a book may not have been the best idea I have had. But it has been necessary for my recovery. Thanks to all who cheered me on? It has been hard to accomplish but I have persevered and accomplished it. Thanks to those who acknowledged my limited typing abilities but helped keep my spirits up and push forward on my own. Somehow they knew the exercise would be good therapy and rewarding for me.

I am grateful Nancy and I found the Alpha program at Saint Benedict's Church in Clayton Park, Halifax in the winter of 2017. It was a Godsend. We learned about the grace of God and Jesus, found a few new friends, and it also helped me to think positive again. Thank you to all who sat at our table, those who gave speeches on overcoming life's hardships and positive aspects in their lives, and thanks to all others who just smiled at us.

During the writing of this book I have learned to forgive my mother. I ask God to forgive her also for the abuse she gave me as a child, and gave us as children. I will not forget, we will not forget, and that is ok. I ask God to forgive her and invite her into heaven to be with him. After all, she was only human and humans sometimes fail at being God-like.

Writing this book has been great therapy to help me get through and accept my new life, to overcome my daily obstacles, and to accept living with an ABI. This is the new me, and I have come a long way. I believe I will succeed with a full recovery.

I thank all those who have prayed for my recovery. Thank you, to all those who visited me in hospital and/or at home, and those that took time to make a phone call to me. It is because of your support and prayers, my doctors, and divine intervention that I am still walking this earth today. I am a living miracle, indeed. Thank you all. Others who have not done so well, I pray you will recover.

I am grateful to Nick and Paul, my former co-workers, who talked to me via phone regularly during my first year of recovery. The talked about their projects and asked for my advice, although it probably was not needed. You helped in a big way in my recovery. It was good to keep my brain active helping you find solutions. Thank you.

I am grateful to Nick for taking a day of work and a flight from Newfoundland at his own cost to visit me. It was exactly what I needed at that time. Thank you and God bless you.

Thanks to my workmates from the Vale Refinery project in Long Harbour Newfoundland site team for their kind messages, phone calls and fruit baskets.

I was once a stanch supporter of our Public health care system but now I realize it is in crisis and needs a revamp. There has been so much money removed from the System while the number of people using it is on a steady increase as our population grows older. This is not a winning formula for our public healthcare future. A big thanks to all the health care professionals, like Nurse Bonnie at Nova Scotia Rehab in Halifax, nurse Leslie at the QE II in Halifax. You were truly amazing. Now that you are retired, I wish you all the best and many years of a healthy and happy, well-deserved retirement. Also thanks to the other health care professionals that helped me along the way. The Nova Scotia government has failed brain injury survivors very badly. The Nova Scotia Rehab needs to revamp their recovery system from a one-program-fits-all because it does not work. I am grateful for their effort for my recovery during my stay in rehab, although I felt much better the day I arrived there than I did on the day of my release. The best thing they did for me was helping me understand my condition and future requirements.

I am grateful for the people who prayed for me and to Jesus for answering them. He comforted me in my darkest hours when I needed it the most. Thank you all.

I have always said that home is not a place, it is a feeling. There is a feeling of being home, contented and happy. I have not felt like I was home for a long time but recently I have begun to feel like I am home. It is a good feeling and I am grateful for that.

I am grateful to my four-year-old granddaughter, Charlotte, who makes me smile every day even when I do not feel like it. I apologize for the past couple of years of your young life. I was not able to be a real Papa to you like I wanted to be. I was unable to chase you around the living room, I could not lift you into my arms or babysit you to allow your mom to have some alone time. I was not able to read you stories like I wanted to, take you for ice cream, take you to the playgrounds as often as I wanted, or to just spend some alone granddaughter and papa time, just to hear you laugh. I believe you and I really missed out, but even for such a young child you seemed to understand. Thank you so much for understanding. You are Papa's princess.

I am grateful to all who purchased and or read my book. Thank you from my heart and soul. I appreciate your support and pray for God's blessing for you. I ask that your lives will be touched with his blessings and favour.

I am grateful to my children, Stefan and Suzanne. They have been so supportive and checking on me daily via a phone call and visiting as time allows them to.

# CHAPTER FORTY

Threading the Needles of Life is not easy. Most of the time it can be difficult. Even in good times, I had the occasional set-back, as most do. Life goes well sometimes, but not often it seems. It is difficult to thread the eye of a needle, maybe it is because the eye does not see what the future holds and neither do we. Our life journey will take us down a dark road where we do not know what lies in wait for us. We do not know the location of hills we will have to climb, do not know how low our valleys will be to climb out of. We do not know the changes of direction that lay ahead, where the sudden sharp turns are, those turns are the sharp curves that life throws at us unexpectedly. They will come at some point in all our lives, not necessarily in old age, but most likely when you least expect it. We do not know if, where, or when our journey on the road of life will end but we think about it often, how it will happen. Will it be slow or be sudden? We do not know. Not knowing does cause us some anguish, but we travel the road as far as we can, with all the will, courage and strength we can muster. We have no choice if we are to survive. To live, we push on no matter what, to get as far down the road as possible. Humans have a will to live as long as possible like no other being on this planet we call earth.

When I look back I see pain, loneliness, insecurity, and lots of heartache and fear. Going forward I see strength, laughter, love, compassion, using the lessons I have learned to do better, and faith in God and Jesus. I am here to leave his world a better place than when I arrived here.

All of us can change our world by writing a new slate and we can help others change their world if we choose to. Tomorrow is not written yet, it is a blank slate, a blank page. So what are you going to write on your slate tomorrow? The choice lies with you. It can be the first and best day of the rest of your life. God gave us freedom of choice, and the choice is yours. What will your choice be? I pray your choice will be to renew your faith in God and Jesus and to show love and kindness to your fellow human beings. Give with your heart and not for recognition, God knows what you are doing. Giving to folks that need it and random acts of kindness will always be your guide to a heart of love, kindness, and bring you closer to your God.

If you want to make a real difference in this world of ours, you have 168 hours each week to do it. Make each hour count with your new choices. Get to it. Each day can be like being reborn again. Make an effort to make this world a better place than when you found it. You can do it. Let go, spread your wings and soar like an eagle.

It is the autumn of 2017 and I am grateful and happy to say Nancy and I have stuck together through all of the adversity. She is an amazing woman. We have come through some very difficult times and we believe we deserved better, but our love for each other has grown, our bond is so great. We are currently planning our lives together, we will make it.

2017 autumn. My perspective on life has changed dramatically these past couple of years. My legs are feeling better than they have since the stroke, but I still have a lot of muscle stiffness all over my body. That, too, will sub-side eventually over time, and life is looking better and better as time goes forward. I have renewed enthusiasm for life.

**Nancy and George prior to George's health issues**

**My daughter Suzanne**

**Nancy overlooking the Gatineau Hills in Quebec**

**George prior to the health issues standing on the shores
of the Atlantic Ocean near St Anthony Newfoundland**

**View of Mortier Bay Newfoundland
near where George was born**

**My Granddaughter Charlotte smelling her favourite flower**

www.ingramcontent.com/pod-product-compliance
Lightning Source LLC
Chambersburg PA
CBHW051441050726
47593CB00005B/1880